Jane -

Let your light
shine! ☼

So glad to have
you as a new friend!

Chris Sopa
3-25-14

Choosing the Life You Were Born to Live

How Changing Your Thoughts Will Change Your Life

Christine Sopa

BALBOA
PRESS

A DIVISION OF HAY HOUSE

ISBN: 978-1-4525-5691-8 (sc)
ISBN: 978-1-4525-5692-5 (e)

Library of Congress Control Number: 2012914757

Balboa Press books may be ordered through booksellers or by contacting:

Balboa Press
A Division of Hay House
1663 Liberty Drive
Bloomington, IN 47403
www.balboapress.com
1-(877) 407-4847

Balboa Press rev. date: 09/19/2012

"*You were born with potential.*
You were born with goodness and trust.
You were born with ideals and dreams.
You were born with wings.
You are not meant for crawling, so don't.
You have wings.
Learn to use them and fly."

~Rumi

Dedication

For my Daddy, Gary G. Morth

Even though you are no longer physically here,
your presence lives on in me through
the words written here.
I love you!

Testimonials

In *Les Miserables*, Victor Hugo explains that prayer is simply a communication between the infinite without and the infinite within, and the reader in a moment sees a truth that is at once obvious and astonishing. There are many such moments in the new book by Christine Sopa, *Choosing the Life You Were Born to Live: How Changing Your Thoughts Will Change Your Life*. Ms. Sopa explores the barriers that keep us from overcoming the fear and inertia holding us back in our lives, and how to use the innate powers of the human mind to achieve joy in a difficult world. The stories from her life, told with great intimacy and wisdom, are more than compelling (and often amusing) anecdotes. They provide a framework, along with many evocative quotes, to lend tangible structure to the lessons learned, methodologies and techniques offered to achieve fulfillment in life. There is also a pervasive sense of metaphysics and spirituality, simply and honestly put forth, that is reminiscent of the late M. Scott Peck. Ms. Sopa's excellent book, told with such vulnerability, feeling and fearlessness, is itself a metaphor for growth and self-actualization.

Dr. William S. Prins, Rocket Engineer
and Author of *Legends of the Ebu Gogo*

Chris Sopa shares her journey to joy with her readers through the masterful art of story telling. As you read her funny, painful, and fascinating stories, you gain insight into your own self-discovery and your journey to joy and the life you were meant to live. Her sharing allows you to discover new truths about yourself! Come along for the journey – you will be glad you did!

Dr. Patricia M. Buhler, SPHR
Professor
Goldey-Beacom College
Author of *The Employee
Satisfaction Revolution*
and *Human Resources Management*

TABLE OF CONTENTS

PREFACE

The book that you are about to read has been in the works in my mind for some time. It is a culmination of life experience, education and teachings from other mystics that I hold dear to my heart. It is meant to inspire you but also to assist you in applying the ideas you learn into your life so you can live the life you are meant to live. My intention in writing this book is to offer you guidance in the process of understanding what you are meant to do while you are on this Earth and learning to use the circumstances in your life as a classroom to move you closer to your purpose.

In my travels around the globe, I encounter many individuals who are stressed, out of balance and have lost the passion for their dreams. They are reacting to life instead of responding to life and wonder why they can never achieve what they want. They feel trapped by their employment, personal responsibilities at home and at the whim of what others think they should do with their lives.

In today's world especially, many are feeling lost and overwhelmed. We are all experiencing a sudden increase in "speed," so to speak, in our lives; losses that are unexplainable and changes abounding in all directions from our businesses, to the economy, to changes occurring within ourselves that we are trying desperately to understand.

There have been many experiences in my life within the last several years that have caused me to live my life from a more symbolic perspective rather than so literally. What do I mean by that? Think of it this way; when an event in your life occurs you can choose to "react" to it or "respond" to it. It is all a matter of perspective. My perspective is that everything happens for a reason. We sometimes are given the gift of knowing what that reason is and other times we are asked to live on faith that although we are not meant to know it, what happened was for our highest good. When we can learn to look at our life through a different lens, one of hope rather than despair, our entire world changes. One of the most significant events for me was the rare experience and honor of being able to take care of my father as he was dying of cancer.

In March of 2006 my father was diagnosed with last stage prostate cancer. He had an aggressive form of cancer which started in his prostate and went undiagnosed long enough that it metastasized to his bones. What was interesting about my father's cancer was that to look at him, you would never know he was sick. As a matter of fact, the only thing that even sent him to the doctor was pain in his left arm. He began, over a few months, to notice that he was having a hard time putting his left arm into his coat. Of course, we all thought this was some kind of bursitis or joint problem. He went to his family doctor and they put him through a battery of tests; blood work, cat scans, x-rays, tests for his heart, etc. They found nothing. Finally, they did a bone scan. That was when they found it. Cancer all down his left arm, into his shoulder, his back, his hips; just about everywhere.

When we first heard the news, we were numb, to say the least. My father was not a total picture of health to begin with, having uncontrolled diabetes for many years. We discussed with the doctor the options and due to the high level of his PSA the doctor wanted to get his hormone level down close to zero before he started any chemo or radiation. Their solution was a pill he would take every day at 7pm along with a mega-dose shot of the same medication he would come to the doctor's office and receive every 12 weeks. Every 12 weeks they would monitor his PSA level to see if this "hormone therapy" was working.

My father went on for the next 8 months with a fairly normal life. Taking his pill, going for the shot, not telling anyone he had cancer. He had hope unlike any hope I had seen, tinged with a bit of denial. His PSA level got "down" to 18 from a staggering 880. He was obviously not out of the woods.

It was shortly after Christmas of 2006 that things began to go down hill. I remember going with him for his routine 12 week blood screening. When the results came back this time, his PSA was in the high 400's. The tumor in his prostate was now out of control and large enough that it was pressing on his bladder and other vital organs. Radiation began. One week later, he was in the hospital for a week being treated for his uncontrolled blood sugar and severe dehydration. That is where they found out the cancer had moved to his skull and brain. A droopy left side of his face caused me to ask the doctor in the hospital to check it out. After an MRI, which he hated due to the fact that he had lived through Vietnam, it was found the cancer was in his skull, the bones of his face as well as the dura (or covering) of his brain. More bad news. Then radiation started the following week on his head. After only two treatments, back in the hospital for another week.

Living in Maryland, I found myself traveling to Cleveland every other week and staying one to two weeks at a time to help my mom take care of my father and talk to doctors. I found myself trying to run an international business from the hospital lobby, raise two teenage daughters long distance, keep my relationship with my husband healthy, sitting in on Board of Education meetings (which I was the VP at the time) on the phone long distance, as well as bring money in since I was the sole income provider for my family at the time (my husband having lost his job of 7 years in December). All of this and trying to deal with the fact that my father, one of my best friends and confidants, was dying a very painful death.

The day I found out about my father's cancer in March of 2006 (I remember the moment vividly…sitting in my black Mazda with my friend Renee having just spoken for a group of women in Philadelphia and getting the call from my mother), I made a promise to myself. I swore that no matter what, I did not want my dad's life to end and look back and say, "I wish I would have…" I vowed at that moment to go to visit him in Cleveland any free chance I had and to say things to him I had always wanted but never did because I felt I still had time to do it later. Every 2-3 weeks I was in Cleveland visiting. I remember at one point my mother asked me why I was visiting so often and proceeded to tell me to stop because I was scaring my father. I was able to spend some quality time with my father and was a key player in his journey to the other side.

I was scheduled to take a 3 week spiritual journey to Peru from March 18th through April 7th. I battled and battled with myself about whether I should go or stay, knowing my dad's condition and that he did not have much time left. I talked to my father and did some soul searching and knew, for some reason, I had to go on the trip. I said my goodbye's and took off for Lima on March 18th. I spent three wonderful, spiritual, sacred, healing weeks in Peru talking with my father when I could, involving him, in spirit, in all of the healing ceremonies I took part in with the native shaman. I knew that the work I was doing in Peru was helping him in some way.

On April 7th, 2007 while standing in the airport in Cusco, Peru I was tapped on the shoulder by our driver Carlos and told I had a phone call. My heart sank to my stomach. It was my husband Jim. I had told him to use that number only in the event of my dad's death. That morning my father had passed away in the Hospice Hospital in Cleveland. I remember standing there in the middle of the airport, dazed yet also relieved his painful journey was finally over. Ironically, my friend Michele who I had just met on the trip was standing next to me when I received the phone call. Michele and I had spent many hours talking about our fathers. Michele had brought with her to Peru a cross from her dad's funeral that she buried on Apu Ausangante while we were hiking. I knew my dad had waited until April 7th to make his final journey. He knew I was worried that if anything happened to him while I was gone I would not be able to get back in time. I could not get back any faster that day then I was already getting back. He knew that. I had made my peace with him more than once and my work in Peru helped him conclude his journey back home.

I remember in Peru realizing that his life was based on *his* spiritual contract. That no matter how much I wanted him to heal and stay with me here on Earth, that the Universe had a different plan for him, one much greater than mine. There was a moment while in Peru I began to pray for his healing, but not in the sense I had before. This time it was not for his physical healing, but for healing that would allow him to fulfill his contract. Healing that would allow his journey to go smoother. His death was that healing I had prayed for so hard in Peru.

He had told me over and over again he did not want anyone in the room when he passed. He wanted to be alone so we would remember him alive and not dead, and he wanted it to be fast. He was so tired he could not imagine dragging this process out any longer. The morning of April 7th my mother called him in the hospital and asked him when he thought would be a good time to visit, that morning or later in the afternoon. My father proceeded to tell her he was feeling good and to go ahead and go grocery shopping that morning and come afterwards. According to the nurses, he was sitting up in bed. He hung up the phone with my mother; the nurse took his blood sugar and then left to get his medications. Twenty minutes later when the nurse returned, my father had passed away. Alone and fast, just how he wanted it. His journey here was complete.

As I, along with my family, went through the grieving process, I realized for the first time how difficult it is to lose someone you love so much. I began to receive "gifts" in the form of friends, books, guidance and synchronistic events, all sent to help me along the way. I was watching others, like my mother, have a hard time dealing with the loss and noticed how different we all chose to grieve. I also realized there were others who never allowed themselves to get through the grieving process, but got stuck along the way. I watched myself go through the ups and downs of the process, not even realizing I was going through "the process."

This book is my journey, my lessons and the guidance I received while I was going through (and still go through to some extent) the grieving of the loss of my father as well as the lessons I have learned from the pain of some of the many other journeys I have taken so far in my life. One of the things I noticed over the last couple of years was how the grieving process is relatively the same no matter what type of loss we are going through. My hope is that the words in this book will help you or someone you love get through the process a little easier, confirm that you are not alone and heal your heart so you know the external essence of the one whom you loved is gone, but his internal essence remains here with you today and to help you understand how to learn from change, loss and adversity in order to empower yourself to live into your choices fully every day.

As you read this book, I will be using the words "Universe" and "God" interchangeably. Please feel free to substitute these words with whatever words fit your beliefs and vocabulary. It is not the words that hold the power (they are simply letters on paper), it is the message behind the words that will heal. I want this message to be delivered to you in whatever form you are most familiar and comfortable with so the full meaning behind the message fits in the context of your soul and understanding. Take this book to heart. Listen to the words with your heart rather than your head. Trust what comes up for you as you read. Be in a state of awareness and allow whatever feelings come up, whether they be joy, tears or gratitude, come up and let them out. Remember, you have to feel it to heal it. Let it be. Allow yourself to be where you are instead of constantly searching for something or someone outside of yourself to make you joyful. Learn to be your own coach and find the tools that work for you and use them. This book is meant to be a beacon of light for those yet to go through, going through or gone through any kind of loss due to death of a loved one, an illness, a lost relationship, a lost job, a thought pattern you have had for some time, or any one of the many things that touch our lives that cause us to stop and change. It is meant for you to seek when you are down, crying, feeling hopeless and feel you have nowhere else to turn. It is meant to be a tool in giving you actual "tools" and things you can do, such as changing your thoughts, to allow you to step into a different place in your life. Let it be your beacon of light to guide you as you take your journey and learn your lessons. Let myself and those mentioned in this book, hold the torch ahead of you, to light the way and carve the path so your journey is bathed in the light of the wisdom and knowledge of those who have gone ahead of you in this journey.

Live the life you were born to live. We are waiting for you.

Your Lightworker,

Chris

CHAPTER ONE

HAVE YOU FOUND JOY?

"Just in case you ever feel its absence....know happiness always returns."

Something's wrong...we feel it...we know it...we're not happy...we're not fulfilled—or perhaps we think we're happy, but our body, through sickness, tells us something else.

Most of us know when we are unhappy, most of us know that we're not fulfilled; maybe we have some comforts—a family, a career—and yet we sense that's not enough, there must be more.

The Ancient Egyptians believed that when we die and are at the gates of heaven, we are asked two questions:

1. Have you found joy in your life?

2. Has your life brought joy to others?

I have noticed that the majority of people immediately know the answer to the first question. This, of course, depends on the ease in which they have lived their life thus far. The second question tends to be a little more challenging. How do we know if we have brought joy to someone else? Is it based on whether or not they like us? Is it based on whether we made them smile? Would we have had to change their lives in some positive way by something profound we said or did? Many of us then start to question our own state of joy at this point. Have I really found joy? Is joy the same as happiness? Then the ultimate question comes: Is joy what God is looking for us to experience?

Although this may sound fairly simple, many people have a very hard time finding joy in their lives. We get caught up in work, family, and household responsibilities, caring for aging parents, financial obligations, and the list goes on and on. Before we know it, our lives are running us and we are just along for the ride. We start feeling as a prisoner in our own lives. A life in which we consciously created every step of the way with things we *swore* we wanted. Fears get in the way and we begin to allow those fears, not our dreams, to dictate the direction of our lives. It is through the experiences we have in our lives which we learn our greatest lessons.

As adults, we learn in three principal ways:

- *Impact moments*, which are events that happen outside of us that jolt us into a specific realization that changes our lives somehow. September 11th was an impact moment for many of us—whether we experienced this event by actually physically being there, watching it on television, or knowing someone who was directly impacted by this event. This event sticks out in memory because it triggered a deep emotional cord in many people that caused them to change their thinking and possibly their behaviors about our country, the people who live here, and most importantly, their individual personal life stories. Many have never been the same since this impact moment occurred.

- *Discovery moments*, which I jokingly call "V8 moments" (imagine yourself hitting the palm of your hand on your forehead) which are self-discovery moments that happen for no apparent reason and just seem to hit you out of the blue. A friend of mine, who suffered with alcoholism his whole life, one day woke up, drank his usual bottle of liquor for breakfast and as he went to get dressed and tie his shoes, his distended liver kept getting in the way and preventing him from bending over; it hit him then that he was going to die soon if he did not change his behaviors. He immediately made a phone call and was in an AA meeting that afternoon.

- *Spaced Repetition* is the one over which we have the most control. Here's how the human brain works: If we hear, see, or experience something over and over again, it gets recorded due to that repetition. Our brain says, "Hey, this must be important because it keeps coming up! I better remember it!" The brain does this regardless of whether the experience is good or bad. We are all very familiar with this one because this is how all of us learned our times tables and it is the main reason why most of us over 40 can recite by heart what is on a Big Mac! Affirmations are a form of spaced repetition. Telling your mind over and over again what you choose for it to believe will eventually (with the fuel of truly feeling and believing it) reframe that belief. Choosing what runs through our minds is one of the most powerful tools we have for transformation. In order to do this, we need to have a basic understanding of how the mind works.

CHAPTER TWO

THE BATTLE FOR YOUR MIND

"Whatever thoughts, beliefs, opinions, theories, or dogmas you write, engrave, or impress on your subconscious mind, you will experience them as the objective manifestation of circumstances, conditions and events. What you write on the inside, you will experience on the outside."
-Joseph Murphy, The Power of Your Subconscious Mind

YOUR CONSCIOUS AND SUBCONSCIOUS MIND

The mind is powerful. Depending on your experiences, you can choose to overuse your mind, ignore it completely, or learn to find a delicate balance of using your mind as a tool as your heart leads the way. We have only just recently tapped into approximately 10 percent of how the mind actually works. That means we don't know about 90 percent of the functions of our mind! The mind is basically divided into sections. For the purposes of our discussion here, we are going to discuss two of them: the conscious and the subconscious.

Your conscious mind is your filter. It is your center of choice. It is that part of your brain that has the ability to choose whether to accept or reject any bit of information that enters your awareness. Let's say I gave you a compliment and you choose to reject this compliment, mentally saying to yourself, "I know that is not true, she is just saying that to be nice." That choice (or thought) then travels to the subconscious mind. Now here is the rub: The subconscious mind can only ACCEPT the information it gets from the conscious mind. It does NOT have the ability to choose! It assumes that what you choose in your conscious mind is what you want. Your subconscious mind cannot decipher between what you want or don't want, what is good or bad, right or wrong, happy or sad, positive or negative, etc. It assumes that what enters from your conscious mind is *the truth.* So now, this thought of rejection has entered the subconscious mind. The subconscious mind expresses itself mainly through your behaviors. Over 90 percent of your behaviors come directly from this part of the mind! (Scary thought for some of us!) How does this rejection thought then express itself? Every thought that we have generates a feeling, and as we will discuss in much detail later, everything in life, every choice, and everything we choose to do or not do is based on how we feel. This feeling then drives an action. The thought of, "She is just saying that to be nice" (or truly what this person is saying is, "I am not good enough,") generates any one of the following feelings; disappointment, doubt, worry, blame, discouragement, anger, jealousy, insecurity, unworthiness, fear…is this sounding familiar? Now how you act on any one of these feelings is up to you and your past behavior patterns. Some will eat, some will take their anger out on a family member or friend, some will sleep, some will zone out with a meaningless activity that sucks their life away (such as watching hours upon hours of TV to take them out of their own reality so they don't have to deal with their lives), and others will push the feeling down until it needs to find a way to release itself and it turns into something physical, such as a migraine, IBS, or back pain. All of this stemming from a thought.

THOUGHTS BECOME THINGS

"We can only do what we think we can do.
We can only be what we think we can be.
We can only have what we think we can have.
What we do, what we are, what we have, all depend on what we think."
~Robert Collier

Once you realize that what you hold in your mind you eventually hold in your hand, experiencing joy in your life will become something you create everyday of your life. Most of us let whatever thoughts show up in our minds take over us like a blanket covering us on a cool night. We remain on autopilot allowing life to throw us around like a ball in a pinball machine. We need to learn to choose our thoughts just as we choose the clothes we are going to wear every day. Which ones fit? Which ones make us feel good about ourselves? Which ones bring out our best qualities? *Your thoughts are your choice!* Anything that you see in the outside world was once a *thought* before it became a *thing*. Before you make a thing in your body, you must make it in your mind first. If you hold a thought about something long enough, you draw it into your life. The problem is, most of us do not hold the thoughts of what we want long enough for them to manifest before we allow thoughts of worry and fear to creep in. Your thoughts need to change if you want your world to change.

THE VEIL AND THE LIES

We all walk around with a "veil" of sorts that masks our true reality and who we really are. Many people are having more and more awarenesses about their lives than they have ever had before. This is truly a remarkable time in history to transform yourself into the person you want to be!

The other part of the "veil" is your own personal one that is created by all of the conditioning and "lies" we have told ourselves throughout our lives. Some of these "lies" sit in your subconscious mind and you are unaware of them as of yet. You only become aware of them by observing your behaviors.

A client of mine, who has been divorced for many years and has had a run of bad luck dating abusive men, recently had a breakthrough during one of our coaching sessions. As we began to dig into why she kept attracting abusive men into her life, I asked her the question, "If you knew, in this moment, you were worthy of unconditional love, what would you do differently?" After much discussion, she realized that her definition of love equaled being "used and abused" and that she felt in order to be loved she had to "earn her worthiness" by "doing what the other person wanted" (let them borrow money, have sex, sacrifice her time, etc.) or they would "go away"…much like her mother "went away" emotionally, due to mental illness, when my client was a child. Although, logically, thought patterns such as these make no sense and you know consciously that what they are saying is not true, our experiences tell us differently. The veil masks the truth and the pattern then lies to us, thus affecting our choices and our behaviors. This client had also been sexually abused by her father at a very young age which is why her pattern concluded: "If I am not being abused then I am not being loved." By re-defining love as something that did not need to be "earned" but something she was worthy of by just being her true authentic self, she was able to change the energy around the type of people she attracted into her life. This affected all of her relationships in a positive way, from the type of men she attracted into her life all the way to how she interacted with her clients.

As you see with the example of my client, many of these "lies" we tell ourselves have come from experiences we had in our childhood. Remember how I said that the conscious mind is your "filter." Well, the conscious mind is not fully developed until around the age of seven years old. If that is the case, I want you to think about all of the events you saw, heard, and experienced before you were seven years old. Now think about all of the things you probably experienced that you don't remember before you were seven years old! All of these things bypassed the conscious mind (because it was not completely formed yet) and went directly to your subconscious mind. You had no say in it whatsoever. Some of those things your subconscious mind thinks are "truths" are actually "lies" and your behaviors and attitudes are living them out on a daily basis. Better yet, your subconscious mind interpreted those "things" from the mind of a child, and when it comes to those things in your life today, it still thinks and acts like a child.

Then there are the "lies" you are aware of and yet choose to continue to live them out. Why do we do this? The reason is fear, which takes many different forms: not knowing what you want, afraid of making the wrong choice, worried about being "selfish" or what someone else may think, etc. The key to changing your life is to bring to your awareness as many things that are getting in your way of becoming the person you want to be; you can then make a different choice. Sounds easy, doesn't it? Being aware of something in your life is harder than you may think. Once you are aware of something, you are then *personally accountable and responsible* for whether or not you change it AND for your behaviors and their consequences up to this point in your life. That is a jagged pill for many of us to swallow! It is so much easier to play the victim role and blame someone else for our shortcomings in life. It is *their* fault I can't do what I want to do, it is *their* fault I have no money, it is *their* fault I am in this awful relationship! And as long as *they're* not doing anything to change *your* situation, you continue to live out your lie, getting all the attention you want and need to feed your ego and keep you right where you are: the very place you do NOT want to be anymore! Every time you talk about, think about, and, most importantly, feel with a passion these victim and blame thoughts, your subconscious mind goes, "got it!" and starts to act on what it thinks you want—which is to be a victim. Because, of course, that is what you just told it you wanted. That is your truth.

Until you become aware that the pain in your life is solely due to YOU, change will not occur.

LAYERS OF AWARENESS

Awareness has many layers—and like an onion you sometimes have to peel them back. One awareness usually leads to another, than another, than another. Sometimes there is a certain lesson we have to learn first before something comes to our awareness, a sequence that sets us up to be able to make the highest choice possible for our own good. Something does not come to your awareness until you are ready to change. Of course, change is always your choice. Remember that the Divine does not give you anything you cannot handle; so if you become aware of something, you can definitely handle whatever choice you have to make to change it.

Phase 1

The first phase of awareness is what I like to call the *"If I ignore it, it may go away"* awareness. This is when you become aware of something and you are just not quite ready to take the steps needed to make any changes yet. Fear runs you at this point and you are living from a place of "what ifs?": What if it doesn't work? What if I lose everything? What if he/she leaves and I am alone? What if no one agrees with me?

Did you ever wonder why every time we think "what if?" we assume the absolute worst? Why can't we for once say, "What if"….and have it end with something magnificent? In this phase, the awareness is sitting in the back of our minds, constantly reminding us that we need to change this thing in our lives. Not only does it sit in our minds, but the Universe lends a helping hand as well: Other people start talking about this "thing"; you see it on Oprah; you read it in a book you are reading at the moment; you pass a billboard on the highway that is talking about it; and your mother brings it up in conversation. Any awareness is a sign from the Divine that it is now time to change this "thing." How long you stay in this phase is up to you, but I will tell you that you are not meant to stay in this phase for very long, nor are you allowed to without some serious consequences.

About nine years ago when I was in the corporate world, I became chronically ill. Now, at the time, I was convinced it had to do with stress, but now I know it was the Divine calling me. Nine years ago was when I became seriously ill, but the universe had really started to call me 20 years ago (some of us are slow learners). Although this process started 20 years ago, it did not reach my awareness until I was in the corporate world.

Here was my life in a nutshell: I was working 50+ hours a week, traveling every month, raising 2 daughters, trying to maintain a marriage, volunteering for every organization under the sun, and getting my Master's degree full-time in the evening—and I am sure there are many other things I have left out. My plate could affectionately be called "a platter." And as we all know, when a platter becomes too full, what happens to the platter? It cracks right down the middle. At this time in my life, I was miserable. I was in a job I hated, on the road way too much, not happy in my marriage and scared to do anything about it, eating a horrible diet and never getting any exercise, and mentally believing that everyone was watching my every move and I had to be "perfect"—a sure recipe for disaster. I knew I was miserable...I was at least aware of that.

There were so many things in my life though that I thought were "wrong" and not what I wanted, I seriously did not know where to start. When humans "don't know where to start," we inevitably all do the same thing...*nothing*. I figured if I ignored my life, my feelings, and my desires and just kept trudging along on automatic pilot, everything would eventually work itself out. After all, I got this far in life without thinking about it and I was not dead, right? So that is exactly what I did: I kept going, and going and going...just like the Energizer Bunny. And eventually, even the Energizer Bunny's battery wears out.

Yet, I had this nagging feeling in my gut the whole time that I was "forgetting something." I kept feeling as if there was something I should be doing but I had no idea what it was. This feeling, when it presented itself, was always followed by a low-level anxiety, akin to when you are anticipating something but are just not sure when it is going to show up.

Phase 2

The next phase of awareness is when you have now realized something has to change but are just not sure what to do about it. As I continued my charade of being the Energizer Bunny, it was becoming more and more clear that something—anything—had to change. (Plus, I really did not look good in pink!) I began to develop some serious digestion issues that were getting worse by the day and extremely inconvenient to my schedule. I ignored them for as long as I could until they became unbearable; finally, I went to my doctor who proceeded to send me through a battery of tests to tell me I was "stressed" (surprise!) and had a chronic case of ulcerative colitis.

Ironically, I did not think I was stressed. When we are on automatic pilot, no matter how miserable we are, that is our routine, our life… that is our normal. I have a cousin who at 28 years old had to have a quadruple by-pass. Heart disease runs on this side of the family and has historically hit the males at a young age. He was aware of this history as well as the fact that his health was probably not stellar for a 28-year-old—not mentioning the fact that he smoked, drank, and rode a motorcycle. I remember him saying shortly after his surgery that he didn't realize this is how "normal" felt. His normal was high blood pressure and all of the symptoms that went along with this, such as pain in his chest if he exerted himself too much, and headaches. He, of course, was aware that for a 28-year-old this feeling may not be normal when he compared himself to his friends of the same age, but the awareness was not enough to cause him to want to change until it hit him personally and physically. I always say that when all else fails, that is how the Divine gets our attention…through the physical.

Perception is reality and as I was becoming aware of my "stress" level and how it was affecting my life, I realized that my perception of someone who was stressed was a visual of a person twitching with frizzed-out hair. Not me…or so I thought. I distinctly remember my doctor telling me I had to take some things off of my plate and thinking to myself, "There is nothing at all that can come off!" I felt I had to do it all and if I didn't, someone else would surely screw it up. I felt the world would end if *I* did not do it!

In this phase, you are faced with a serious choice. You can take the time to figure out what needs to change or, as I did, continue to ignore it. Fear is the one and only thing that keeps people held in this phase. Fear is simply *False Evidence Appearing Real.* It is an illusion that we have built into a monster in our minds that is running the show.

FEAR

One of the things I commonly find no matter where I am in the world is that people are all the same. We all have the same fears, anxieties, and worries and we all seem to think we are alone in feeling those things. Our fears come from past experiences, past lives, and witnessing other people's experiences in the hopes that they don't happen to us. The only way to conquer fear is to face it, look it in the eye, and let it know you know it is there. Once light enters darkness it is no longer dark. This is where you have to be honest with yourself. What are your fears? What takes away your power? It could be a person, a thought, a place, a situation, etc. You need to know where your shadows lurk if you want to be conscious.

In May of 2009 I decided to take a solo journey out west for two weeks. Since my divorce in 2008, I have really enjoyed traveling alone. Many people think I am crazy, of course. I frequently hear things such as, "A woman shouldn't travel alone!" "Aren't you scared you will get lost?" "Who do you eat dinner with?" and "Why would you even want to travel alone?"

The truth is, yes, I was a bit afraid to travel out west alone. I flew to Grand Junction, Colorado, rented a car and drove over 3,000 miles to Seattle. Along the way, I stopped for some intensive hiking—*all alone*—in Moab, Utah; Border, Nevada; and Mount Shasta, California. It was not being alone that I was afraid of. We all need to be able to enjoy our own company and, to really get down to it, like ourselves. What is a bit scary is when we embark on something new that we have never before experienced. It is the fear of the unknown that gets us. Letting fear stop you from experiencing life's adventures is a true tragedy. Fear is simply an illusion. We create fears in our minds, expand them and make them "real," going over and over the worst possible future scenarios in our minds. This way of living is living your fears, not living your dreams. Never, ever let fear stop you from doing something you love, something that will bring you joy, and something that will help you grow into who you are meant to be.

Phase 3

The last phase of awareness is not a pretty one. Not everyone has to get to this point to change, usually only us stubborn ones or people who have had certain patterns running their lives so long they could swear the "off button" was stuck! In this phase, the pain of where you are and the choices you are making becomes greater than any fear of changing. At this point, you don't care if you are alone, living on the street, hungry or naked in front of a thousand people...you have to change or you feel as if you are going to die!

This is the point where you finally take action.

I was married for 16 years—graduated from college at 20 years old one Saturday and was married the following Saturday, 6 months pregnant and moving to a city in which I had never lived before (in fact, I had never moved from the town in which I grew up). I had both of my daughters by the time I was 23 years old and knew the evening of my wedding night that the bliss into which I had just entered was not going to last. Not wanting to go home and admit that I had "failed," I decided that this was the choice I made and I had to make the best of it. I continued along with my life, enjoying raising my girls and pretending to be happy in an empty marriage. By the time I was 32 and was hit with the ulcerative colitis diagnosis, I had battled endometriosis, constant severe abdominal pain, migraine headaches, and a very close call with cervical cancer. I would find out later after healing myself of ulcerative colitis that all of these ailments had to do with not honoring myself and finding the truth in my life.

It wasn't until after my father died in April of 2007 that I finally began to see life from a new perspective. My father was the most joyful man I knew. Seeing my father walk around the house singing out loud and putting our names in the songs he was singing was commonplace if you visited the Morth household. My best friend Judy reminds me frequently of my dad walking down the hallway in our house singing, "I Am the Warrior" by Patty Smyth at the top of his lungs. As the cancer took hold of this compassionate and loving man, he began to go within himself and not talk, sing, or interact with those he loved anymore. He looked frightened and scared and always seemed to be intensely thinking.

One day I got up the nerve to ask him if he was afraid of dying, assuming that is what was going through his mind. I will never forget his answer. He looked at me and said, "Chris, I am not afraid of dying. But when I think of all of the life I didn't live that I can never get back now, that is what gets me."

From that day forward I chose to live by the oath that I never wanted to get to the end of my life and say, "I wish I would have…." I began to make the choices in my life based on this pledge. When I found myself worrying about something I would ask myself, "Will I be thinking about this on my deathbed?" So, if paying the credit card bill was not something I would be thinking about on my deathbed and I was spending my energy worrying about it, I would immediately stop and shift my energy to something that was more important. We have three choices when it comes to something we are concerned about: Change it, leave it or accept it as it is.

I had always trusted that when it was time to leave my marriage I would know; that day came in July of 2008. I could not imagine living the life I was living anymore; I felt as if it was no longer a fit for me. The pain of staying became greater than the fear of being alone. I was finally ready.

THE DESIRE FOR CHANGE

"The way the Creative works is through change and transformation, so that each thing receives its true nature and destiny and comes into permanent accord with the great harmony: this is what furthers and what perseveres."
~ I Ching.

We never know when we are going to get a desire to change our lives in some way. Sometimes it is due to a life-changing experience and other times it may just present itself out of the blue, a way of God waving the red flag for us to see our highest path.

Dolores Hart, a prominent actress from 1947-1963 who played opposite actors such as Robert Wagner and Elvis Presley, had such an experience. Having grown up in Hollywood with both parents being

Hollywood actors, Dolores always had a passion for the stage. After starring with Elvis Presley in *Loving You* in 1957 she became a very in-demand actress. In 1961, she was cast as the role of a nun named Clare in the film *St. Francis of Assisi*, which filmed in Rome. While in Rome, she met Pope John XXIII and this completely changed her life. After introducing herself to the Pope as "Dolores Hart, the actress who plays Clare," the Pope prophetically responded, "No, you ARE Clare!" Eventually, Hart left the acting business and became a nun and is currently the Reverend Mother Dolores Hart, the Prioress of an Abbey in Connecticut.

Mark Wahlberg, the well-known actor in movies such as *Invincible, The Fighter,* and *We Own the Night,* was also able to change his life, although the "calling" came from within. Addicted to cocaine and at one point charged with attempted murder, he was in trouble with the law 20-25 times as a youth and eventually landed in prison. He then started to make different choices. *"It wasn't until I really started doing good and doing right by other people, as well as myself, that I really started to feel that guilt go away,"* Wahlberg said in an ABC news interview. *"So I don't have a problem going to sleep at night. I feel good when I wake up in the morning."* Now Wahlberg is a committed Roman Catholic and has a charitable organization called the *Mark Wahlberg Youth Foundation*, which is dedicated to youth services and enrichment programs.

It doesn't matter in what circumstances you find yourself that create the desire to change; what matters is the actions that create the change. We are all human and mistakes are a part of being human. Messing up in life is what makes us who we are. Our mistakes are nothing to feel guilty about because they are the vehicles from which we learn our greatest lessons. It is not the mistakes that matter; it is how you respond to those mistakes in the end that makes all of the difference in your life...and as in both cases above, makes a difference in the lives of others as well.

CHAPTER THREE

OVERCOMING LIMITING BELIEFS

"Once you become aware of a belief that is limiting you in one way or another, you then have the power to change it."

WHAT IS A BELIEF?

Beliefs are funny things. For some beliefs, we feel very strongly, and are prepared to sacrifice our lives to defend them; other beliefs run the very essence of our behaviors and yet we are still unaware of them. Our beliefs are simply the thoughts we allow to run through our minds.

The majority of our beliefs were formed before we were seven years old. If you recall, this was when our conscious mind was not yet completely formed and most of what we saw, heard, and experienced made its way directly to the subconscious part of our brain. These beliefs take the form of what we believe as far as religion and our spirituality, how we view and what we believe about others, and most importantly, how we view and what we believe about ourselves. Our beliefs give us the blueprint with which we interpret and then respond to the world around us. When it comes to beliefs, people like to be right. They will hurt with their actions and words to defend their beliefs. We see many examples of this in our society but we also see examples of people using their beliefs to promote good as well.

WHERE DO OUR BELIEFS COME FROM?

As we grow up, every single thing we experience with our senses conditions us. Our past conditioning is formed without our consent or permission. It lays itself in the recesses of our minds to form the "rule book" for how we will make choices in our lives going forward.

As much as we would like to erase some of our past conditioning, it is there to stay. We cannot get rid of it even if we desperately wanted to. Our conditioning sits in our subconscious mind, and as we go about our daily lives, a button is pushed, if you will, that stimulates some past conditioning, which in turn triggers a thought. The thought is a conditioned response as well because it is very much connected to the belief that was formed by the conditioning we received. Some of these thoughts help move us forward and some of them hold us back. Regardless of which direction our thoughts take us, every thought leads to a feeling. It is these feelings that trigger an emotional response that dictates how we choose to react to any given situation in our lives.

The biggest place where our conditioning threatens us is in the view we hold of ourselves.

"Everything you think about yourself, everything you believe about yourself, is because you learned it."
~Don Miguel Ruiz

We have formed our own opinion of ourselves based on what we heard others say about us throughout our lives, especially in our younger years. We believe about ourselves what we perceive other people believe about us. We take it all in—every word, every look, every bit of attention or lack of attention—and make it our truth. The problem with this is that the view of others—including their view of you—is formed through their own lens of the world and what view will most benefit them, not you. This is why it is critically important to identify those beliefs you hold about yourself and the world around you that are limiting and holding you back from your true potential and divinity. You need to come up with your own beliefs that match what you want in your life and the type of person you want to become, and that are not based on the needs and prejudices of others.

"Everything in our lives can wake us up or put us to sleep, and basically it is up to us to let it wake us up."
~Pema Chadron

It is safe to say, knowing from where most of our beliefs came, that most of our beliefs are not even ours. They are the beliefs of our parents, friends, teachers, society, television, and even to some extent, what we are still holding onto from our past lives that has buried itself in our subconscious minds. Of course, we periodically question "our" beliefs when we are faced with adversity; but do we question them to the point of really making sure they fit into the person we are and want to become? Do our beliefs support our highest path and the highest path of the whole of humanity? After all, that is why we are here.

One of the strongest beliefs people have concerns their spirituality. What someone believes about God has caused arguments, wars, break-ups, and lost lives. Our spiritual beliefs, for most of us, were introduced to us when we were little. We went to church with our families, we listened to them have conversations, and we watched their behaviors.

I grew up Roman Catholic. We went to church every Sunday and on holidays, we gave up something we cherished for Lent, and we believed that Jesus was the Son of God brought down to earth to suffer for our sins. As I grew up, went to CCD every week, and listened to the sermons from the priests at mass, I was taught not to question God. We were not allowed to ask questions about why something was how it was; we were just supposed to blindly believe it because that is what it said in the Bible. As I became an adult and began to travel to different countries and make friends that had very different spiritual beliefs, I began to see and feel that what I was brought up to believe didn't make sense to me. It wasn't that it was right or wrong, but for *me* it didn't feel right and fit into my new beliefs and what I was experiencing. I learned very quickly that other people felt very strongly about their own spiritual beliefs and for some reason always seemed to try to make others wrong if someone else's beliefs did not match their own. We all do this to some extent with beliefs about which we feel strongly. I guess our reasoning is that if it makes sense to me then why doesn't it make sense to you? What we forget is that each one of us came from very different backgrounds, very different experiences, very different conditioning, and very different environments.

Our beliefs and experiences dictate how we react in any given situation. When I was in South Africa in November of 2009, I went on a safari, which was one of the most amazing experiences of my life. During the last hour of the safari, a thunderstorm kicked in. If you have never been on a safari before or experienced a storm in the middle of Africa, it is unlike anything I can even explain. The lightning appears as if it is striking the ground right next to you and the rain is coming down so hard it actually hurts when it hits your face and body. Not to mention that you are sitting in an all-metal jeep and there is no place to go for cover! Once our guide realized the storm was imminent, we observed his actions begin to change dramatically. He had experienced one of these storms before and knew the dangers. My friend and I did not. Our experience of a thunderstorm was quite different. As Sam, our guide, began to drive frantically to get us back to our bungalow, my friend Tina and I were laughing hysterically in the back seat. We were having a good ole time experiencing the storm because we were unaware of the danger we were in. Our belief about storms differed dramatically from Sam's.

We made it safely back to our cabin and the next morning found out that the storm's lightning had killed the largest bull rhino on the grounds as well as struck the house of the owner of the resort and burnt it to the ground: a humbling experience to say the least.

I recently dated a man who was Lutheran. He was brought up to believe in the Bible as the word with no exceptions. He and I fell madly in love with each other and had a blissful relationship for about 3 months. Once the novelty of new love wore off, things began to change; or at least that was my perception. To be fair, let's say the energy shifted dramatically. Out of nowhere (in my opinion, of course) he no longer wanted to have a physical relationship and felt that our spiritual beliefs were too far apart to see each other anymore. Although he was not completely clear on his beliefs and did have times where he questioned them, he felt he needed time to figure them out and did not want me around while he did that due to the large gap in our beliefs. Needless to say, I was devastated. I could not understand, if he loved me, why we could not respect and live with the differences we both had around spirituality. In the end, he felt so strongly about his beliefs that he chose to honor those beliefs rather than continue the relationship.

In the end, someone can never go wrong if they are being true to themselves, whether they are sure of their beliefs or not. The beliefs we have now are all that we've got. They may change or take a different form in our future, but they are what we use to make our choices in the moment and we must honor them.

We are not what we believe we are. We are so much more and we can create a new belief and a new us every day if we choose. Becoming aware of the lies we are telling ourselves—that are in the form of beliefs that are limiting us—is the first step toward a "new" you.

"We need to remember we are not our bank account, we are not our relationship, we are not our profession, we may not even be whom we have been conditioned to believe that we are. Don't believe everything you think. You can create a "new you" every day of your life."
~Don Miguel Ruiz

According to Teilhard de Chardin, our job is to proceed as if limits to our abilities do not exist. Limiting beliefs are like spells. They captivate our thinking and we are not even aware of it. They change our feelings, actions, and behaviors and then they influence other thoughts. Our thoughts and actions do not just influence us, but those around us. We listen more with our eyes than our ears. People form their opinions of us by watching our actions. If our actions are not in line with what we truly believe and who we truly are, then what people experience is a false sense of who we are. People then observe us and form their opinion about us based on false actions. It becomes an endless cycle that at times we feel as if we cannot get out of. It brings a whole new meaning to feeling like a hamster on an endlessly spinning wheel!

The truth is we have inside of us all of the knowledge we need to become who we were meant to become in this lifetime. This knowledge becomes hidden behind conditioning, false beliefs about what we can and cannot accomplish, emotions, and other people's opinions. The key is to become aware of the thoughts that are holding us prisoner and break through them once and for all. We need to take the time to identify who we are and what *we* want based on our new found beliefs.

"Our challenge is to forget what we have learned and remember what we have forgotten."
-Adam, "The Path of the Dream Healer"

WHAT DO YOU WANT?

"We were not born to get stuff done — we were born to dream it and move toward it."
-Esther Hicks

Seems like a simple question, doesn't it? What do you want? We have been asked this question hundreds of times in our lives. The funny thing is, not many people can truly answer this question. The classic answer I hear when I ask this question is, "I want to be happy." Those who have worked with me know it is at this point I begin to go into a convulsion! I simply look at the person and say, "Go deeper!" Is there anyone out there who doesn't want to be happy? When it comes to identifying what you want in your life right now, be as specific as you can. What is it that makes you happy?!" This is the point where I get blank stares. The answers are all things outside of themselves, such as, "If my kids are happy then I am happy"; or they start to list accomplishments of everyone else in their lives that will make them happy.

The majority of people have no idea what they want. They allow life to push them around and just react to what life offers them instead of choosing what they want out of life and demanding that life delivers that to them. We need to learn to respond to life rather than react to it. Two very different things. Reacting comes from the subconscious mind and it is the automatic behavior that is elicited from a conditioned response to a situation. For example, if I grew up in a household where yelling was the preferred form of communication and how you got someone's attention, my reaction to a situation where I wanted to get someone's attention would be to yell. It would be automatic. Unless, however, I learned that yelling was inappropriate and did not necessarily get me the results for which I was looking; then I would re-learn a new behavior to get someone's attention. When the next situation comes up where I want to get someone's attention, I would slow down and choose my new behavior instead. I would *respond* instead of *react*. Responding involves engaging the conscious mind to override a habit in the subconscious mind. It is being aware moment-to-moment of what is going on in your head and around you so you can choose the response that is in your highest good.

DREAMS

Most people have a very hard time deciding what they want. Our wants come from our dreams. What has happened is that we have learned to squash our dreams before we even allow them to grow in our minds. We say things such as, "I don't have enough money," "What would people think," "I'm too old to do that," etc. Many of these thoughts are due to past disappointments of wanting something in our lives that never showed up when or how we wanted it to. We take these experiences and form a generalization in our minds that nothing we want will ever manifest. Then, after a while, we stop dreaming altogether, which is the main reason people do not know what they want.

One of the saddest moments I can remember as a facilitator was when I was working with a group of teenagers at an alternative school on this topic. I asked them to get out a piece of paper and start writing down some of the things they wanted in their lives: their dreams. After a moment of hesitation and no one writing anything down on their papers, I asked them what was wrong and why this was so hard. One of the students stated, "Why should we bother to dream. Dreams don't come true anyway!" I had to fight back the tears that welled up in my eyes before I answered this student because I was so taken aback that a group this young had already lost their passion to dream…their zest for life!

Our dreams are where it all starts for us. Everything we see around us was once someone's dream. They are the basis for what we create in our lives and the groundwork for the choices we make. Dreaming is like a muscle that we have forgotten how to use and must learn to use again. We need to be able to dream so we know what we want and can then focus on these things so our life becomes what we want it to be.

It is critical to be able to define what you want. Remember how earlier we discussed how your brain works? We make a choice in our conscious mind and then that choice is delivered to the subconscious mind. The subconscious mind then acts on our "want" through our behaviors. It sends out signals, if you will, to the Universe telling it how to line up to deliver to us what we want.

Another important reason why it is important to know what you want has to do with your fears. Limiting beliefs are thought patterns that hold us back, that limit us in our thinking and our actions. Normally, when we become aware of a limiting belief or a thought that does not make us feel good, our first response is to just not think about it anymore. We ignore it thinking if we do this long enough it will go away. Here is the rub. Our brains do not work in a vacuum. We cannot just identify a negative thought or pattern and eliminate it and leave a blank space where that thought used to be. We have to replace it with something. We have to change the old habitual thought to a new, more positive one that works in our favor. In order to replace this old negative thought, we have to know what we want so we know with what to replace the old thought or belief.

AM I SELFISH?

"Responsibility is not defined as an obligation to care for others excluding your own self."
~Caroline Myss

The most popular response I hear when I ask people what they want is, "Isn't that selfish to talk about what I want?" Let's get this out of the way right now! Everything in life has to do with intention. Intention is what you hold in your heart as the reason why you are doing something. Truly selfish people have a misguided intention that they are the only ones that matter and they intentionally do things without any regard for other people and how they feel. When we are focusing on ourselves with the intention to make ourselves a better person, to feel better, and to grow that is anything but selfish! The better you are as a person the better you can be for everyone in your life, for those you love. Those who love us want us to feel good and be happy just as you want those you love to feel good and be happy. By disregarding yourself, you are doing a huge disservice to the ones you love: You are stripping them of the opportunity to feel good because they see that you are content and enjoying life. What you do for yourself ultimately benefits others!

SHOULD'S

Our lives are dictated by "should's." We seek advice from friends, family, and loved ones when we are distraught and they tell us what we "should" do. Asking for help comes from a place of forgetting... forgetting we have a voice. I am not saying you should not ask for help. If we were meant to do this thing called life alone we would not have been all put here together. We just sometimes forget that our own voice is important too. We listen to our own voice so little that most of us don't even hear it anymore when it is softly calling our name.

Writing this book, for instance, is a great example. This book has been four years in the making and over those four years I have been seeking advice from editors, publishers, friends who had written books, famous authors…all who told me what I "should" do. Every bit of advice was good, but not my own. Every bit of advice was given from the heart with my best interest in mind, but not from my heart.

The more I heard, "*Shouldn't* your book be done by now," "You *should* try to work on it every day," "You *should* try to set a goal of when you want it done," the more I hesitated, procrastinated, and sank deeper into questioning myself as to "why" it wasn't done. This even lead me to question why when I sat down to write, nothing came to me. After all, I am an inspirational speaker. Ask me to speak on a topic and I can go on for hours. Ask me to put on my coach's hat and coach one of my clients and brilliant things come out of my mouth. Sit to write about it: nada.

I just recently saw the movie, "Eat Pray Love" with a friend. As I watched Julia Roberts play the part of Liz, I was reminded blatantly of my own life, as I am sure were many women. The similarities were shocking. Listening to the message of the movie I heard myself over and over again saying the same things, teaching the same lessons to my audiences and clients. Seeing a book by a friend of mine cross the screen when Julia Roberts was buying books at the bookstore at the beginning of the movie made me stop dead in my tracks; I was flooded of course with more should's as to why *my* book wasn't done yet.

I realized how every aspect of our lives is connected. If we are "off balance" in one area, it filters into the other areas, whether we like it or not. I have been divorced now for 4 years. Do I regret any of it? Of course not. I have two beautiful daughters and a lifetime full of lessons that have made me who I am today. Being young, I made the best decisions I could make for where I was at that point in my life. I left my husband because I felt like I had lost myself somewhere in the house, kids, being a wife, cleaning, PTO, etc. I didn't know who I was anymore and felt as if I needed permission from someone, not sure who, to be myself. Without that permission, whenever I did anything for me, I was swarmed with guilt and regret.

Having been on my own now for 4 years, I have finally found myself again. I have grown a successful business, traveled extensively alone and with friends, and cried many tears of regret, forgiveness, and gratitude. Until just recently, I had been questioning why every area of my life seemed complete except in the romance department. Ironically, I even signed up for one of those online singles dating sites only to find that after 4 days my self esteem had taken such a hit I wondered why I was even bothering in the first place!

Watching "Eat Pray Love", I had one of those impact moments we sometimes have that we never forget. In every relationship I have had my whole life—every single one, including my kids and friends as well as romance—I have felt as if I needed to give up who I was to please the other person: In essence, become who they wanted me to be so *they* could be happy. I was caught up in whom I thought I *should* be. I was constantly putting someone else's happiness over my own. Caroline Myss calls this the Rescuer archetype. I call it self-masochistic behavior! Even though I talk openly about wanting my highest spiritual partner to enter my life, pray about it, cry about it, and, many times, give up on it, I realized I am subconsciously keeping that "Mr. Right" away due to a fear of losing myself once again to another human being. After all, based on my past experiences, if I share my life with someone that means I lose a part of myself, right? I have to sacrifice something of me to give to them. Sounds romantic doesn't it? The line that brought me to tears in the movie was, *"Sometimes you have to be out of balance in love to have balance in life."*

I always know when I hit one of those moments that are life-changing because on the whole drive home I did not turn the radio on once. I was in deep meditative thought. Cried some, laughed some, but most of all felt a sense of relief I have not felt in a very long time. I finally felt free! (Thanks, Liz Gilbert!)

That was the moment I realized I could write this book. I have a story to tell and most of my story is about releasing the fear to finally live my life. It's about learning that life is here to enjoy, not to suffer through, and that we are here to live our dreams and not our fears. We all have a divine right to that joy. There is not one exception.

GUARANTEES AND CERTAINTY

"So many people live within unhappy circumstances and yet will not take the initiative to change their situation because they are conditioned to a life of security, conformity, and conservatism, all of which may appear to give one peace of mind, but in reality nothing is more damaging to the adventurous spirit within a man than a secure future. The very basic core of a man's living spirit is his passion for adventure. The joy of life comes from our encounters with new experiences, and hence there is no greater joy than to have an endlessly changing horizon, for each day to have a new and different sun."
-Aron Ralston, "Between a Rock and a Hard Place"

One thing that holds us where we may not want to be is needing a guarantee that things will be ok—that everything will work out how we want it too, that we won't be hurt, that we will still have a paycheck, etc. Sometimes when we "don't know" how something will turn out, that is exactly when we need to go to our hearts and stay out of our head. It is like trying to apply logic to heaven. It cannot be done or understood from our human perspective. Where is your focus? Is it on what you want or on what you don't want? Where your focus goes, energy flows… so be careful what you are holding in that mind of yours.

I have found in my life that there are no guarantees, there are no certainties in life. As humans, we thrive on certainty. We take very calculated risks only after we have researched, done a pie chart, and discussed it with all of those whose opinion matters to us to see what they would do. Certainty is, in my humble opinion, based in fear. When we want certainty, we are trying to control the situation due to a fear that it will not turn out as we want it. What if we don't get that job we want so desperately? What if I quit my job and start my dream business but make no money and cannot pay my bills? What if the man or woman of my dreams never arrives and I am alone the rest of my life? What if this disease takes my life?

The truth of the matter is, our potential lies in uncertainty every time. Uncertainty is where our divine contract waits for us. It is where the highest potential of our being calls us to—gently at first, and then, once it knows we are listening, it shouts so loud to draw us near to it that we abandon all logic and reason and flow with life in the direction it wants to take us. This is how we manifest. This is how we live from the heart and abolish fear.

I have a client who tells me all of the time, "Chris, I think there are only two emotions: love and fear." I believe he is right.

YOUR 7 IMPOSSIBLE THINGS

"It's kind of fun to do the impossible."
~Walt Disney

One great way to see where your fears lie is to bring them up in your mind for a brief moment in time so you can shed some light on them.

A wonderful exercise I have my coaching clients do is to list seven things in your life you want so bad but are scared to death will never happen: Your "Seven Impossible Things." Why seven? Because seven is a very sacred number and there is a certain power in having to force yourself to think of more than just three or five things. You have to go deeper into your mind and deeper into your fears.

The key to the exercise is to list the seven things you want and then walk through all of the reasons why you think it won't happen…what you fear will get in the way of it happening. Then, in a column next to it, list all of the reasons how it *could* happen.

For example, one of my seven impossible things is to move out west. This has been something I have wanted to do for many years. My list looks something like this:

Why this won't happen...	How this CAN happen...
My daughters live east	My daughters can visit me out west
I don't have enough money to move	Believe the money will manifest exactly when I need it
My business was established in the east	I travel all over the world to speak so it doesn't matter where my business was established
Most of the people I know are east	Travel west a few times a year for business or pleasure to network and meet new people
My credit score is not good enough to find a place to live	Rent a place and pay cash or use my debit card for all purchases and take steps now to mend credit report
My car won't make the trip	Rent a U-haul and haul my car instead of driving it
My family lives east and in Ohio	Plan to visit family a few times a year and invite them to visit me out west
I don't know anyone who lives out west	See above
What if I am dating someone and they don't want to move out west	Trust that I will meet someone who is willing to move or already lives out west
I will miss my family too much	Use Skype to keep in touch and visit family as often as I can
I currently do not have any clients out west	Use LinkedIn and people I know to help me prospect new clients out west now

When you take the time to really think through and put on paper your fears and then possible solutions to those fears, the fears lose their power. The fears turn simply into obstacles that can be easily overcome with a plan and a little faith. You then are also focusing on what you want to have happen instead of all of the reasons why it cannot happen, using the power of your thoughts to manifest exactly what you need. Thanks to my list above, I am currently in the process of moving to

Arizona. I have since bought a new car (which I am towing behind a U-haul), found a roommate to live with so we can share expenses and save money, and have since acquired new clients out west. Do I still have some fears? Sure; but the actions I have taken eliminate the fears to the point that excitement takes over, because the obstacles all have a possible solution!

Having a plan, such as the one above, is one of the ways to overcome fear; another way is to understand and know that Divine is there to help you on your journey. You are never alone.

CHAPTER FOUR

THE POWER OF CHOICE

"We did not come here to make choices. We already made our choices.
What we are here to do is to learn to live into our choices
and understand why we made them."
-The Oracle, "The Matrix"

Choice is the most important gift we have been given in this human incarnation. Free will to *choose* what we want to experience and what we want out of this particular life is truly a gift. I find it hard to fathom how some individuals do not believe that they can create their own reality: If this were not the case, why would God have given us the will to choose?

Having this gift requires responsibility—the responsibility to be aware of the highest, best, and most thoughtful choices. Not just the ones that benefit us personally, but the ones that benefit mankind as a whole. Choice implies conscious awareness. That is why becoming aware of what is limiting you is the first step. Once you are aware of something, you now hold that awareness in your conscious mind. It no longer sits in your subconscious mind, hiding and masking itself as fear. You now are conscious of it, which means you now have the responsibility to do something about it, to make a different choice.

"All we have are the choices we make, one at a time. And from such choices are created larger events of humanity. It is simply up to each of us to trust that every choice we make matters."
~Caroline Myss

We can try to avoid making choices by doing nothing, but even that is a choice.

WHY IS IT HARD TO MAKE A CHOICE?

As we have discussed, we ultimately have 3 choices when we are faced with any challenge in our lives: Accept it, change it or leave it. Why is it sometimes so hard to make a choice? Because we let one thing and one thing only get in our way: FEAR! All of our fears stem back in time to an event that caused us some kind of pain. Once we understand that fear resides in our minds and is an illusion, we can overcome it.

Carol, a 44-year-old woman, was diagnosed with a very rare genetic disease that affected the amygdala of her brain. One of the key roles of the amygdala is in making people feel afraid in threatening situations. Fear does serve a purpose. It warns us, just as pain does, when there's something to which we need to pay attention. It is when we take it too far and make choices based in fear that the problem occurs. Carol lived her whole life without fear. Her brain did not record conditioning as a normal brain did. When she was blasted with a loud horn every time she saw a blue square, the sight of the blue square in the future brought up nothing—no fear or remembrance that a loud horn sound may accompany it. For those of us with a normal brain, the sight of the blue square would trigger a conditioned response of fear that something bad was about to occur, even if we didn't remember it was a loud horn—and even if there's no horn anywhere around. This is how our brain works. It records everything we experience, regardless of the logic surrounding it.

Fear and conditioning affect our choices. When I got divorced, I remember being afraid of being alone for the rest of my life and not having anyone with whom to share my journey. This fear kept me rooted in my marriage for a long time. It was a choice I made based on the fear of being alone. Once I finally conquered the fear of being alone by facing it and taking action *despite* the fear, I realized that being "alone" was extremely empowering. It allowed me the circumstances and the opportunity to get to know myself again and step into the person I was meant to become. The only limitations we have in life are self-imposed. Nothing stands in your way other than your belief around a certain situation. Whether you believe you can do a thing or not, you are right.

"You are like a railroad switch. Each time an event occurs, you channel the activity onto the positive or negative track. Even though the event hurt you or took something away from you, you are still in charge of channeling it onto a positive or negative track. You determine its future outcome."
~Unknown

Whenever I have a choice to make, I ask myself two questions: *What are the consequences of this choice that I am making?* and *Will this choice bring fulfillment and happiness to me and also to those who are affected by this choice?* Then I immediately go to my heart and see how the choice "feels." If a good feeling comes up, I move forward. If a not-so-good feeling comes up, I wait. This process helps me make the "right" choices each time. This way, even if I do not get the result I expected, I know that choice I made in the moment was the right one. The result does not matter; only the feeling at the moment you made the choice matters. The result is up to the Divine. The choice that feels right in the moment leads you to the highest result every time.

Every day we have a choice to choose our attitude and beliefs. On my journey out west, I remember waking up some mornings feeling extremely tired and not wanting to continue to drive hundreds of miles, or to hit the hiking trails again; but I did it anyway and chose to make the best of what I had been offered that day. When we do this, we choose to LIVE! We choose to be our best no matter what the circumstances of our life situation. That is what life is really all about….living no matter what! We create our lives as we go along. It is our responsibility to make it the best life we can while we are here.

"You have choice. You can select joy over despair. You can select happiness over tears. You can select action over apathy. You can select growth over stagnation. You can select you. And you can select life. And it's time people tell you you're not at the mercy of forces greater than yourself. You are, indeed, the greatest force for you."
~Leo Buscaglia

CHAPTER FIVE

BELIEVE IN YOURSELF

The main reason most people decide not to change their lives when they know a change is in order is due to the fact that they feel as if they do not "deserve" good in their lives. They feel guilty for their mistakes, regret their actions, and for some reason feel as if they now deserve to suffer for the rest of their lives. How we treat others is a direct reflection of how we treat and feel about ourselves. It is the perfect mirror. Before we can believe in others, we first need to believe in ourselves.

SELF-LOVE

"Love yourself, accept yourself, forgive yourself and be good to yourself, because without you the rest of us are without a source of many wonderful things!"

If I were to ask you if you loved your children, you would more than likely answer with a very rapid "Yes!" Don't you find it funny that we can so unabashedly love an extension of ourselves but not love our own selves?

When we think of the love we have for our children, we know we love them because of how they make us feel. We would do anything for them, no matter what. We would give up anything for them. Make any sacrifice for them. We want the best for them and do whatever we can to make sure they have the best life possible. You know when they are sick or not feeling well because your "mother/father instincts" tell you so. You know them so well that you know what they need, what their moods mean, and when they are just plain tired or hungry.

Just for one minute, I would like you to be your own parent. Treat yourself as you would that child you love so much. What would you do first for *you*? What do you need right now?

If you find it hard to answer these questions and to know what to do for yourself, you are lacking self-love. We do not take care of that which we do not love.

If I were to tag one area where almost all of my clients have a similar missing link, it would be in the area of self-love. When I ask them to do a Bucket List of things they want in their lives, I get a list of things they want for their spouses, children, and friends. When I ask them to take some time during the day for themselves, even if it is just for five minutes, I get the guilt response of "I don't have time" every single time. Funny how when our children need our time we find the time but when *we* need the time, there is no time. I ask all of my audiences to ask themselves this question: "If you treated your friends like you do yourself and if you said to your friends what you say to yourself, how many friends would you have?" I always get a gasp from the audience at this point. You know the answer.

I have wondered often about how we get to the point where we lose our love for ourselves. We are born with it. We are born with the Divine knowing that we are important, lovable and worthy. What happens? Where does it go?

Over our many years of living, we allow people, things, thoughts, and places to take our power. Every time we allow something into our thoughts that takes away a little piece of us and makes us think we are not important enough to have love in our life, our power has been taken. We know this has happened by how we feel. As soon as you have an interaction with someone or something and it makes you feel "bad," you know you have lost your power. You could lose your power to a specific person, money, a job, an actual place, a thought pattern…you name it. Every time you allow your power to be taken, you lose a little bit of self-love. Balance is not letting anyone or anything love you more than you love yourself.

Self-love is THE most important thing you need in this life. In order to have self-esteem, which we will discuss later in detail, you need to love yourself first. You cannot hold yourself in esteem until you love yourself. The question becomes, once you lose it, how do you get it back?

The first place to start is to get to know yourself again. What do you like to do? What makes you feel good? What is it that you do where you lose all sense of time because you enjoy it so much? Do those things! Do them as much as you can!

Next, develop a routine where you take time out each day, preferably the same time every day, to do something for you that is mental in nature. Say certain positive affirmations, meditate, do a chakra cleansing visualization and stick to it! The best time for me is right before I get up in the morning. This is my time to briefly meditate, read my affirmations, and channel and get some guidance for my day ahead. This time centers me and honors the fact that I feel I am important enough to spend time on *me* first thing in the morning before anyone and anything else. It sets the tone.

As each day passes and you are slowly learning to love yourself again, remember that your best is different every day. Life is not about the answers you are seeking, it is about the "source" of those answers. Do those answers come from your highest self? From a place of peace, serenity and tranquility in knowing that only *you* know what is best for you? You will make mistakes along the way. Mistakes are what allow us to learn and grow. Don't beat yourself up over them. That is why you are here: to learn from your mistakes. You built the mistakes into your journey so you could see the contrast between what resonates with you and what does not. What choices fit best with who you want to become and who you are now? Our job is to learn to be the observer of our own lives at the same time that we are the participant—to have a healthy detachment from the emotion and to watch the emotion come up but not let the charge of the emotion take over. We always have the choice to respond rather than react. When we finally realize we have the power to respond how we want to rather than how we think others expect us to, then we are on our way to self-love.

SELF-WORTH

"That which you know you are worthy of creates. KNOW you deserve love, kindness, compassion and abundance. Know it. Breathe it. Live it."

We already have spent some time talking about self-love, which is the foundation upon which we build our self-worth and self-esteem. Not feeling worthy to allow yourself to receive the good that naturally is pouring into your life in answer to your prayers is the main block in manifesting what you desire. As we saw in the previous chapter, our lack of self-worth often comes from the thought patterns that take us in the wrong direction. You make your choices based on what you feel worthy of receiving. If you want your choices to come from a higher place, you need to increase your self-worth so it is coming from a higher place.

Once you feel worthy, you have esteem; this gives you the confidence to make new and different choices; you then begin to lead your life in a new direction which is in alignment with the "new you;" finally, you become an example for others and without knowing it, lead them to a more fulfilling and happy life. Coming from this new place of self-worth, you are now living a life of service by using the example of your own life as a teaching tool for others. Any deed you do for yourself is *never* selfish—because anything that you do for yourself, you are also, indirectly, doing it for others. This is what Jesus' life was all about. He used his life as an example to teach us how we could live. Living from a place of such high worthiness, knowing we are all pieces of the Divine and all connected, *that* is true worship. That is your church. We honor and respect the life God has given us by making ourselves the best person we can be; that is our gift back to God and those whose lives we so gently touch.

Your self-worth comes from inside of you. Your self-worth is not attached to attaining a specific thing or person into your life; it is a mindset that you create in accordance with how you feel about yourself. No one, and I mean *no one*, controls the strings to how you feel about yourself. You are the only one who allows them to have that power over you. How you feel is your responsibility. If someone says something to you that is "negative" in nature, it is your *choice* whether or not you "let it in." It is your choice on how you choose to perceive and interpret that comment. You create your reality! Never undermine your own self-worth by comparing yourself to others or taking in negative things they say. It is because we are different that each of us is special. We each have a specific gift to offer this world and we are the only ones who can deliver it.

SELF-ESTEEM

"FAQs asked of the Oldest Angel -

The Answers Are Quite Simple:

Who am I?
Spirit in a body.

Where do I come from?
The one spark of All that seeds this entire universe.

What am I here to do?
Align & Design; become the creator you already are."

~Reverend Angela Peregoff

Many of us have been brought up in a society where we are told, either directly or indirectly, that focusing on ourselves is "selfish." Too much time spent on YOU is "not a good thing." You *should* focus on others and put yourself last. Does any of this sound and feel familiar? With these thoughts swimming around in someone's head, no wonder very few people take the time to nurture themselves and work on their own inner self-image.

Why is building self-esteem so important? When you feel good about yourself you feel as if you can do anything. When you believe in and trust yourself, everything is possible. A positive self-esteem gives you permission to be who you were put here to be. Permission from whom, you ask? Permission from you! You are the only person from whom you ever need permission to move forward in your life. No one, and I mean no one, has the right to take away your power and tell you that you cannot do something with your life! We give our power away to other people in this area all of the time. We do it due to the fear we innately have of worrying about what others think of us. Sometimes this fear gets out of control and we give "control of the buttons" to others (sometimes people we don't even know) to run the show. We make decisions based on what other people would think versus what we think is best for us. This eventually leads to bitterness, anger and self-destructive habits.

"You wouldn't worry so much about what people really thought of you if you knew just how seldom they do."
–Anonymous

One area of my life I personally have to really pay attention to in regards to my own self-esteem is in romantic relationships. When those little heart strings start to stir because of someone special in our lives, we tend to forget that we are the ones in control. In the past, I always had a habit of adjusting "who I was" to fit the person I was with so they would like me. I would never do this to a drastic measure, of course, but enough that I was not truly being myself. These things would always be what I thought were little things, such as not speaking up if something was said with which I didn't agree, not mentioning a certain thing I liked or didn't like, or just simply holding back my enthusiasm for something we would experience so the person I was with didn't think I was "weird." We are meant to express and be who we are, so when we suppress any part of ourselves, we trigger a stress response within us. We start to become very critical of ourselves, which in turn causes us to be very critical of other people as well. How we feel about and treat others is always a reflection of how we feel and treat ourselves. Our minds start to race and we do not know what is right and what is wrong anymore. We lose who we are in the other person. When we allow this to happen, we lose our center. Our center is that place we can come back to when we are feeling "off" to re-group and get our head back together—or said differently, to remember whom we are. You only have a "center" if you have self-esteem.

Your goal is to get to the point where your self-esteem is high enough that what you think about yourself is more important than what others think about you, no matter who they are. You want to love yourself more than anything else in your world. The world around you could crumble, people could be calling you names or your significant other could decide you are not the one for him/her and leave—it doesn't matter: You are calm in the middle of all of the chaos. Your center is the place where your self-esteem resides. When you are feeling "attacked," your center is the place where you go to remind yourself of who you are, how you feel about yourself, and why you believe the things you do. It doesn't matter anymore who comes and goes in your life and what they say or don't say, you ultimately know how you feel about yourself and what makes you tick. We all need to make sure our center is a healthy place we can go to escape this crazy world of chaos. Your self-esteem is your sanctuary. The place where you can go when all else has failed. When you go there, you know all is good, you are perfect just as you are and all you need is the breath in your lungs and the love in your heart and all will be fine.

One of the reasons why many do not have self-esteem is due to the model our society has created around people who have high self-esteem. This model declares that if you have high self-esteem, you are independent, on your own, can handle your own challenges and therefore...lonely! Many relationships are based on co-dependency. I have a need, you have a need....I fill your need, you fill my need. Done! So what happens if someone comes along with high self-esteem and they have no apparent "needs?" Now what? Now you have an *adult* relationship. One based on unconditional love, strength, and truth. Many individuals feel that they cannot have a relationship unless there is a need to fill. This is where self-sabotaging patterns emerge, such as over-analyzing situations to look for the bad in someone so you don't get hurt, breaking up with someone before they "break up with you," being late for that job interview, and procrastinating doing things you know are important. Having high self-esteem holds you accountable for who you are and the choices you make. It is like being your own parent. Your self-esteem is the part of you that keeps you in alignment with your true self and with what is the highest choice for you at all times.

Self-esteem is truly living by your own rules and not caring anymore what other people think. If what you are doing, saying, and thinking is giving you joy and inner peace, you know you are on the right path. True self-esteem is not having any fear of "doing it wrong" or "doing the wrong thing" because that just doesn't exist anymore. You are just being "*you*" and you finally realize that although it may be different from everyone else and you may "screw up" every once in a while, that just being "you" is enough. You are perfect exactly the way you are and you are exactly where you are supposed to be right now.

Self-esteem is something that comes from within—an inside-out development process. All of the answers you seek are inside: selfless, flawless, and waiting for you to discover them. You have to work on the mind and the feelings first and then use your physical self to support what you have created in your mind. For example, once you make the choice to increase your self-esteem, do something that makes you feel better physically, such as getting a haircut, taking a shower, putting on some make-up, shaving, putting on an outfit that makes you feel sexy, etc. This action alone makes you feel better, even if only for a moment, where you then have a chance to choose a different thought about yourself.

"If you accept your own body, you can accept almost everyone, almost everything. This is a very important point when it comes to the art of relationships. The relationship you have with yourself is reflected in your relationships with others. If you reject your own body, when you are sharing your love with your partner, you become shy. You think, "Look at my body. How can he love me when I have a body like this?" Then you reject yourself and make the assumption that the other person will reject you for the same thing you reject in yourself. And when you reject someone else, you reject him for the same things you reject in yourself."
-Don Miguel Ruiz, "Mastery of Love"

My own level of self-esteem has come a long way. After being brought up in a household where I was told that saying or thinking anything good about myself was "conceited," I had a lot of work to do! I used to be terrified of getting lost if I hadn't been someplace before. Now, I enjoy my own company traveling around the world alone, renting a car and driving to places I have never been (thank you GPS!). I used to be terrified to speak up in front of a crowd. Now I am an inspirational speaker, speaking to thousands of people at a time; more often than not, I have a microphone in my hand.

One way that I found to help increase my self-esteem was alone time. Most of us tend to avoid alone time because when we are alone and all is silent, our "stuff" (our worries, our preoccupations, deadlines and challenges on the horizon) comes up to the surface. Why? Because it sees a non-distracted human being who finally has time to address what needs to be released and balanced in his/her energy field. The main reason so many individuals resist "alone time" is that they know that they will be accountable for dealing with their "stuff." They fail to see the opportunity of alone time. When you are alone, only *you* can take care of you. Only you can entertain you. You finally get the chance to get to know who you really are! No distractions, no other opinions, no interruptions, no chores, no influences…only you!

ALLOWING AND ACCEPTANCE

"There comes a time when you have to stand up and shout: This is me damn it! I look the way I look, think the way I think, feel the way I feel, love the way I love! I am a whole complex package. Take me….or leave me. Accept me…or walk away! Do not try to make me feel like less of a person just because I don't fit your idea of who I should be and don't try to change me to fit your mold. If I need to change, I alone will make that decision. Love me or leave me…but don't steal any more of my precious time judging me….set me free! When you are strong enough to love yourself 100%, good and bad – you will be amazed at the opportunities that life presents you!"
-Stacey Charter

On a trip to Seattle a couple of years ago, I had a day to myself between speaking engagements and decided to visit the Boeing plant for a tour. Traveling alone, as I often do, you tend to gravitate toward others in a group who are also alone. This day, I gravitated toward a wonderful man named Gordon from Scotland. He was on the tour alone as well and we decided to spend the day together, visiting the Air and Space Museum after the Boeing tour. Gordon, having been a retired British Airways employee, had a plethora of knowledge about airplanes and proved to be quite the educational addition to my "day of flight" in Seattle. I wondered a few times to myself why Gordon was alone, as I am sure he did of me as well, but did not feel inclined to ask since he did not bring it up.

On the bus on our way back to our respective hotels, Gordon asked me what brought me out all the way to Seattle by myself. I proceeded to tell him about my career, my divorce and the frequent trips I take alone, concluding the story of how my father passing away is what motivated me to "live life in the now" and to finally truly accept myself for who I am and have the courage to do what I wanted to do with my life. As I spoke, Gordon had tears in his eyes and upon the conclusion of my story, sweetly smiled and said, "This is my first trip alone...I waited 2 years to take it." He proceeded to tell me how his wife of over 50 years, whom he met when he was 17 years old, passed away 2 years ago due to a fast progressing lung cancer. She had found out she had cancer and 6 weeks later passed away, giving Gordon no time at all to prepare for the loss of the "love of his life." He said they had always planned to travel when they both retired and diligently waited, saving their money, until that day. His wife, having died 2 weeks before her retirement, never got to experience the trips she and Gordon spent so many nights talking about. Gordon then looked at me with tears streaming down his face and said, "Chris, I never once imagined that one of us would not be here when it was retirement time. Good for you for living your life to the fullest now...don't wait...you never know what life has for you around the corner."

"Practice the art of allowing yourself. Begin by letting yourself be more spontaneous and less regimented in your daily life: Take a trip without first planning it. Go where you're instinctively guided to go. Tell the authoritarian part of you to take a break."
~Dr. Wayne Dyer

How many times do you hear people say, or maybe you say yourself, I will wait until I retire to do that, I will wait until the kids graduate, I will wait until I have the money, I will wait until I get divorced, etc. My question to you is, why wait? Why not now? Most of the time what I see with my coaching clients as the reason they feel as if they need to "wait" to live their life and do what they want to do is because of the lack of present moment living – i.e. allowing themselves to be "WHO THEY ARE" and knowing that they do not need anyone else's approval to want what they want and to do what they want to do. We always seem to think the future will be a better time to live our lives.

PRESENT MOMENT LIVING

"This is a perfect moment and I am centered in the power of the present."
~Archangel Michael affirmation

I want you to realize at this very moment what you are doing. Yes, I know you are reading this book, but as you read the book is your mind wandering elsewhere? Are you thinking about the laundry you left in the washer? Are you thinking about that email you forgot to send? Are you worrying about some bill you have yet to pay off or is late? If any thoughts are occurring that are taking your attention off of what you are doing at this moment, reading this book, you are not present. Many of us, the majority of the time, are not *here*! We are re-living some past moment or creating in our minds some future event. Being present, or in the "now," is one of the most powerful skills you can master that will bring you closer to the joy you seek. It will help you manifest anything you want in your life effortlessly. When you are present, you are truly here, in your mind, body, spirit, and emotions. You are able to see things you don't normally see, you are able to hear things you don't normally hear, you are able to feel things you don't normally feel. Why? Because all of your power is in the present time! You are able to see the doors that the Universe is opening for you in answer to the prayers you have sent it. The present time, my friends, is where all of the power is to create joy in your life!

Being in the present moment as much as you can is a "present" all in itself. The "present" that presents itself is in the form of the opportunities you will find when you are truly "being here" and showing up for your life. Enjoy the process of life! Remind yourself 100 times a day if you have to, to be present.

As you wind down and allow yourself to be present you begin to feel a bit anxious. This is the ego being afraid to let go of control. The ego imprisons you by keeping you in the past and the future. It does not want you to think about the present because it knows that is where the power of manifesting your true desires lie. It does not want you to be empowered and present, it wants you to be afraid so *it* can be in control.

During one of my trips to Peru, a woman in our group started to cry as we were in the van on our way to hike the Inca Trail. Our guide, Evert, asked her what was wrong and she said she was scared that she would not make it on the trail. Evert looked at her and said, "If we are always thinking in the future, we will almost always be crying!"

"Any form of negative emotion contains a message for us. Negative emotions are no longer needed to signal you what is needed in your life when you reach a certain degree of presence. When negative emotions come up, use them as a sign to be more present. You are more than likely reliving something in the past or thinking about an event in the possible future."
~Eckert Tolle

What happens when you are present is that you become "aware." Awareness is a state of consciousness where something you did not notice before comes into your energy field. I believe becoming aware of things in our lives is kind of like that old saying, "When the student is ready, the teacher appears." I would say it as: "When the student is ready, awareness appears." Once you are aware of something, there is no turning back...you are always, forever aware of it. Yes, of course you can make a choice to ignore it, but it will always be in your conscious now. Nagging at you like a splinter in your mind! (Lovely thought, isn't it?) Our mind is truly an amazing gift we have been given. Although I believe many of us spend way too much time in our minds (we will discuss this later!), it never ceases to amaze me how it works.

"Our entire life consists ultimately of accepting ourselves as we are."
~Jean Anouilh

When you become aware of "where you are now" and allow the feelings, the wants, the desires, and even the fears to come up, you realize that life is short. Life is about living in the now, not in the *tomorrow*. All of the magic is in the moment you possess right now. That is where God dwells, that is where your power dwells, that is where the magic of YOU dwells: in those moments where you realize that it is ok to be who you are, want what you want, and that you do not need *anyone's* approval except your own to do what you want to do with your life. When you realize this beautiful nugget, you then dwell in the space of acceptance. You finally accept who you are, faults and all, and know with every fiber of your being and every beat of your heart that you are OK....just being *you*. The *beautiful you* that you are, unique in every sense of the word and here to bring a gift to this planet that no one else can deliver but *you*.

No matter where I am in the world, one of the truths I have realized is that people are all the same. We all have the same fears, anxieties, and worries and we seem to think we are alone and we are not! Change starts with one individual who makes a choice to do something different, something unique and something to honor the many gifts they have been born to give.

Allow yourself to BE HERE. There is nothing like experiencing the opportunities and synchronicities that show themselves when you are truly in the moment and "being there" for your life.

"I was regretting the past and fearing the future.
Suddenly, my Lord was speaking…
MY NAME IS "I AM"….he paused
I waited…He continued…

When you live in the past with its mistakes
and regrets, it is hard. I am not there.
My name is not I WAS.

When you live in the future, with its problems
and fears, it is hard. I am not there.
My name is not I WILL BE.

When you live in the moment, it is not hard…
I am here.
My name is I AM."

BOUNDARIES

"One of the most unique and beneficial gifts we can give ourselves is to know our own personal boundaries."

As you become empowered, one of the most important things that needs to be done almost immediately is protecting your energy. How do you protect your new-found energy? Personal boundaries. When we hear the word "boundaries" we immediately think about a boundary as something that keeps something or someone *out*. A boundary's purpose is never to keep a person or thing out necessarily but to keep the energy of a specific behavior away from your energy field. It is a matter of what you will and will not tolerate now. It is all about personal space and protection of that which you hold most sacred: You.

In life, we only ever get what we tolerate and settle for and now that you honor yourself and hold yourself in esteem, there are new rules. There has to be "safeguards" in place in order to support and protect the space in which you now operate, keeping it pure and of a similar vibration for that which you want to create.

Your personal boundaries begin in your mind. You need to decide which behaviors from others support the new you and which do not. Some may come to mind immediately. Examples of healthy boundaries include not allowing a particular person to raise their voice to you anymore, not going to certain low vibration places, such as bars or pubs, not consuming certain foods or beverages, and so forth. Others may suddenly appear with a particular situation, and you realize: "This behavior is not working for me anymore." Through your feelings, learn to become aware of when you lose your power and to what or whom. The minute you start to feel "bad" (not in a state of joy) or "in your head," you know you have lost your power. Call it back by taking a deep breath and re-centering. Remember, no one thing or person can make you feel powerless; only you can do that.

The most important boundaries, however, aren't related to outside things and people, but instead are connected to our own thoughts and behaviors. You may want to call these "self-disciplines" rather than boundaries, but whatever you call them, you need them to keep yourself in check and on track. Decide which thoughts and behaviors support the "new you" and which do not.

I decided just recently that one of the personal boundaries I needed to change for myself was in my consumption of alcoholic beverages. I am by no means an alcoholic, but do enjoy the occasional glass of wine or beer when I am out with friends or business colleagues. I noticed, as I continued to do work on myself and my vibration rose higher, that when I consumed any alcoholic beverages I became sick to my stomach or got an extreme headache. When I took on a new behavior with alcohol, I noticed my fear of what my friends or colleagues would think if I did not have a drink with them. My "boundary" was honoring my decision regardless of what others thought or how it made them feel.

Regardless of what boundaries you choose to have—with yourself, with places and things, and with the people in your life—honoring the new you by protecting your "sacred space" is vital to the process of self-discovery. Never undermine the power you have over your own life. You make the rules and others can only have a say if you let them.

CHAPTER SIX

BELIEVE IN YOUR PATH

"Your work is to discover your world and then with all of your heart give yourself to it."
~Buddha

In the one of the last movies of the "Lord of the Rings," there was a pivotal scene I will never forget. One of the main characters in the movie, who was destined to be King by birthright, had been living a life as a ranger, fearful of stepping onto his destined path. A conversation was being had by this ranger and one of the elf elders, and in a moment of desperation, the elder said to the ranger, "There is a time to do what you want to do and a time to do what you were meant to do. Put the ranger aside and become who you were born to be!"

I think many of us, down deep, we know our path. My path is to be a spiritual teacher and healer. How do I know this? I feel it in my bones. Just as if I were to have you close your eyes and touch you with my finger and ask you, "What am I doing?" You would respond with, "Touching me." How do you know I am touching you? You feel it. Sometimes others see our path a little more clearly than we do. My younger daughter is an amazing writer and extremely gifted with poetry in particular. On a long drive one day to visit family in Ohio, she wrote the following poem describing my purpose here:

Savior Please
The one to love, the one to help
Save her from saving you
That's NOT what you are supposed to do
She'll take your pain and make it disappear
Put it in a bag and not let you shed a tear
She saves a million, doesn't leave one
Takes everyone until the job is done
Teaching as she walks through the rugged terrain of life
Making it possible for you to live
Loving many, teaching some
Saving all.

Of course, I wept when she read it to me because it is so beautiful. It perfectly describes what I am here to do…and I know it. I love teaching and speaking. It is in my blood; I would do it all day long if need be. If I won the lottery tomorrow, I would not change a thing about what I do. The key is to find what brings you joy when you do it and then DO IT!

"It is very important that you do only what you love to do. You may be poor, you may go hungry, you may live in a shabby place, but you will totally live. And at the end of your days, you will bless your life because you have done what you came here to do."
~Elizabeth Kubler Ross

Many of my coaching clients become very frustrated because they want so badly to know what their purpose is. They feel as if they are never going to find it and worry that they are going to miss it or are on the "wrong path." An acorn doesn't worry whether or not it carries within itself an oak tree; it is what it is: a seed for an oak tree. Your purpose is revealed to you when and only when you are ready. To feel as if you are living your purpose is a daily journey. After I was sick, I started on a self-discovery process and opened myself up to every lesson life offered me—pain or happiness. I learned to see every person that entered my life and every situation as a learning experience that was taking me further down my path toward my purpose. That journey is still continuing to this day. As you work on yourself, as you are now, it becomes easier and easier to use your intuition and discern your path. Intuition is like a muscle: The more you use it, the stronger it gets. I believe our "purpose" is whatever brings us joy. That may change as our life moves forward, but as long as we stay in a state of awareness of our feelings and our inner truth, we are living our purpose. And when we stray off the path—and we will—our awareness lets us know, through our inner feelings, that we have left the path; immediately, we do what we need to do (or, more likely, we become who we need to become) to get back on the path.

"You ARE your path, so you are always on it."
~Elaine Kempski, Inner Journey Coaching

Everything is connected to feelings. We make decisions based on emotion, not logic. Everything that is in your life right now, from the things to the people, are there because of how they make you feel. When the feeling changes, you change who or what is in your life.

If you could only have one feeling for the rest of your life, what feeling would you choose? Be specific here. Don't just say "happy"—that is too vague. Put some meat on the bone! My "one feeling" is inner peace. I use this feeling to help me make every decision in my life and this helps me stay on "purpose." I ask myself constantly, "Does being with this person bring me inner peace?" "Does working with this client bring me inner peace?" "Does doing this or that bring me inner peace?" You get the picture. Find your "one feeling" and use that as your guidepost, your measuring stick to constantly check if you are on the right path.

"The purpose of life is to matter—to count, to stand for something, to have made a difference that we lived at all."

Make your life count. Do what you love. Don't die with your "music" still in you. You are here to deliver something very unique to this world *and you* are the only one who can deliver it. Trust, have faith, and know deep in your soul that your purpose will find you.

TRUST YOURSELF AND YOUR CONTRACT

"Trust in life and what you need will be there."

Every single one of us has been put here on this earth to enhance our personal spiritual growth as well as play a role in the evolution of humanity as a whole. Those of us who have chosen to be here at this particular time in history asked to be here. We knew, in our soul of souls, that we were equipped to deal with and significantly contribute to what was needed to move humanity forward. We are the "best of the best," so to speak. Our contribution is making a difference in the evolution of the earth and humanity.

As we live our lives day to day, we experience a multitude of things— some good and some bad. We all have an idea of how we would like our life to turn out. We have aspirations, goals, intentions, and dreams, all of which give us the internal motivation to move our lives forward. But more often than not, life throws us a curve ball. We will be plugging along at our life just fine and everything is going according to plan and then the car breaks down, someone we love passes away, we lose our job, someone we love decides to leave us…I could go on and on.

Normally we respond by fighting to get our life back "on track." We say to ourselves, "This was not in the plan!" We struggle desperately to force our life back on the path in which it was headed. What we fail to realize is that those experiences that we curse are the very experiences that we need to get us on the "right" path—the path that is aligned with our spiritual contract.

Caroline Myss in her book, *Sacred Contracts*, defines a contract as your overall relationship to your personal and spiritual power. It is how you work with your energy, who you give it to, and how much you are willing to trust in what you feel. Your contract does not spell out every little detail of your life but it does give you a context of the bigger picture. Think of it like the yellow brick road in "The Wizard of Oz." Dorothy followed her path (the yellow brick road) but the experiences she had along the way to get her to "Oz" were made up of the individual choices she chose in response to the experiences she had along her journey. Each situation she was presented with was one in which she could make a choice that would either get her closer to Oz or further away. Whatever path she chose, she learned lessons along the way that helped her make an even better choice next time. And with each lesson and each new choice, she got closer and closer to Oz.

I have mentioned several times so far to begin to look at your life from an observer point of view. Take yourself out of the emotion and the details and step back and look at the overall picture. Ask yourself, "What is really happening here?"; "Has something like this happened to me before and if so, why does it keep happening?"; "What am I supposed to learn here?" When you come from an observer viewpoint, when you look at what's happening from a higher perspective, you give yourself the opportunity to see your "yellow brick road." Most of the time, we cannot see how what happened to us fits into the bigger picture until it is over and we step back and look at the whole situation. Then we see how each person, each event and each choice played a role in strengthening our relationship to our personal power and divinity.

After a while, you realize that even when things don't go according to plan, they turned out to be the best anyway. You realize that there is a bigger plan that supersedes your plan. Sometimes when a situation looks like it is taking you further away from what you want, it either took you that way to protect you from something or someone or it is a better path for you to learn what you need to learn to get you to your final destination. Either way, you get there.

"You have to give up the life you have to get the life that's waiting for you."
~James Hillman

In my coaching practice, I come across people all of the time who are receiving "clues" that are trying to guide them closer to their spiritual contracted path. Many of them kick and scream because they see the clues but want to stay on their current path because it is "safe" to them. They know the in's and out's, they know what is expected of them, they have the skills they need to complete the tasks, they are making the money they need to make to support themselves and their family, and, most important of all, they are comfortable. Everything seems to be "in control" and they know what outcome to expect. As human beings, we do not like uncertainty. As a matter of fact, we do everything we can to make sure we are certain about how something will turn out. We try to control every situation, and sometimes people, to be sure the outcome is what we expect. So when we are faced over and over again with clues that are trying to pull us away from the path we are on and take us to our higher path, we fight with all that we've got.

A client of mine worked in corporate for over 20 years. She worked her way up the ranks to a VP position, was secure in her job and making pretty decent money. Although she may not always have realized it, she is a person of very high integrity and confidence. She is one of those people who just commands attention when she walks in the room and her presence is very empowering. Working in the banking industry with mostly males, she found that as she rose in the ranks she encountered more and more resistance from her male counterparts; this resistance came in the form of back-handed comments in meetings, having her ideas brushed off, and being overlooked for promotions. When her father became ill, she began to have to work from home and take more time off from work to care for her father. She immediately noticed a change in how her boss treated her. All of a sudden, they announced that they had eliminated her position and let her go with no severance.

My friend, being a woman who had been divorced for 14 years and on her own financially, found the thought of not getting the money due to her terrifying and extremely unfair. She fought tenaciously to get her severance pay, but each effort she made seemed to take her further away from getting what she wanted: the certainty of having money in her bank account while not having a steady job.

After months of battling with the union and a lawyer, she finally realized that maybe the Divine was asking her to take a step of faith and working in corporate was not what she was supposed to do. She always had a dream of starting her own business but was terrified to do so because of an ingrained false belief that she could not make money working for herself. The day her father passed away was the day she launched her own business. She stepped off of the cliff, believing there would be a bridge to catch her or she would grow the wings to fly if she fell. Two years later, she is now the owner of a very successful business. She has had her struggles along the way, as with all of us in business for ourselves, but faith and trust guide her every step of the way. She is living a life she loves and is surrounded by friends who support her and love her…money in the bank or not.

"When you have come to the edge of the light that you know and are about to drop off into the darkness of the unknown, faith is knowing one of two things will happen: there will be something solid to stand on or you will be taught to fly."
-Patrick Overton

Our sacred contracts are written in the heavens. It is how we fulfill that contract that is our choice. We can take the low road, the middle road or the high road. Which one we take depends on which way we choose to turn when we come to that crossroads. Either road we choose, a contract is a contract. Its fulfillment is a guarantee, even if it takes more than one lifetime to do it. We have left ourselves clues along the way in the form of people (what they say, their reactions, watching their lives unfold), synchronistic events and happenings, global events, relationships and the "teachers" they bring, or those simple impact or discovery moments that happen just at the right time in our lives. Even if we are kicking and screaming along the way, the Divine always has a way of gently nudging us back in the direction pointed towards our highest path.

By coming to understand that you are not alone and always watched over, you begin to trust the process of your life. You begin to allow it to unfold without fighting it every step of the way. Our resistance slows down the process. It gets us further away from our path; hence the meaning of surrender. Surrendering to "what is" allows you to put all of your energies in the present moment instead of putting your energy into worrying about the future or fretting over the past. You must begin to foster a belief in a higher power, whatever name you may give it, that has your best interests in mind. The heavens see the bigger picture. They see things we cannot see. So come to learn that if you feel you are being guided toward someone or something, trust that instinct. Go with it. It doesn't need to make logical sense and you don't need to have the skill already to do it. Actually, if it doesn't make logical sense and you don't have the skill, *make sure you go with it* because that is a sure sign it is Divine guidance. How else would the gods keep you listening to guidance if not by giving you something you don't know how to do? Learn to check situations and people with your heart and not your head. Ask yourself a thousand times a day, "How does this feel?" and you will begin to learn the inner workings of your own inner divine "guidance language" that has been waiting patiently for you to hear her. Almost every time you follow your inner guidance, miraculous doors open that you would have never seen if you did not trust in your path…but most importantly, if you did not trust yourself. You are not waiting for the answers—the answers are waiting for you. Stop struggling, relax, and allow yourself to receive the gifts that are being given to you.

In Loving Memory
(a memorial card at my Father's funeral)

Oh, for the peace of a perfect trust,
My loving God, in Thee;
Unwavering faith, that never doubts
Thou choosest best for me.
Best, though my plans be all upset;
Best, though the way be rough;

Best, though my earthly store be scant;
in Thee I have enough.
Best, though my health and strength be gone,
Though my weary days be mine.
Shut out from much that others have;
Not my will, Lord, but Thine.
Even though disappointments come
They too are best for me;
To wean me from this changing world,
And lead me nearer to Thee.
Oh, for the peace of a perfect trust
That looks away from all;
That sees Thy hand in everything:
in great events and small.
That hears Thy voice-
A Father's voice-
Directing for the best;
Oh, for the peace of a perfect trust,
A heart with Thee at rest.

TAKING RISKS

"But risks must be taken; because the greatest hazard in life is to risk nothing.
The person who risks nothing, does nothing, has nothing and is nothing.
They may avoid suffering and sorrow, but they cannot feel, learn, change,
grow, love and live. Chained by their certitudes, they are a slave."
-Author Unknown

Risk. Even the word sends shivers up your spine. We associate so many things with the word risk, most of them negative in nature. We all have experiences of when we took a risk and were hurt or disappointed. We told someone we loved them only for them not to say it back. We spoke our truth in a meeting only to be chastised by the boss. There are a ton of examples, all of which are valid—and all of which caused us pain. But what about the stories of risks we took that did turn out ok? Somehow, when we are faced with a challenge and taking a risk is involved, we only seem to recall the times when we risked something and it *didn't* work.

After healing from my ulcerative colitis, I had a choice to make: Go back to the job that caused me so much stress or step into blank space and start my own business. I remember sitting at my kitchen table contemplating the decision. In front of me sat the mortgage bill for the house my husband and I had just bought; my two girls were in the other room sitting on our comfortable sofa watching television and my husband's paycheck stub was in my hand…not nearly enough on its own to pay all of our bills. We were a two-income family as are most families today. There are times in everyone's life where you can *look* back but you know you cannot *go* back. I was at one of those times. I knew in my soul I could not go back to my current job but what would I do? How would the bills get paid? Starting my own business was a pipe dream—something I knew nothing about or had the first inkling on how to do. I remember thinking to myself, "Ok, you just went through a hell of an ordeal with your health and got through that, what's the big deal?" With money in one hand and my health in the other, I asked myself, "Which one can I do without? Which one is less risky to meddle with?" Hands down I knew that I could not mess with my health again. What good is money if you have no health and cannot enjoy it. I knew that if I went back to the life I was leading before my ulcerative colitis I would surely get sick again. Nothing changes if nothing changes. All I had to do was *think* about my old job and I could feel my intestines start to rumble! Somehow I knew, down deep in my soul of souls, that if I started a business the money would work itself out. After all, I have always lived by the belief that everything happens for a reason. That reason is usually a tool in which we learn a lesson and then as a gift to others, and part of our service here on Earth, we use that lesson to teach others how to better live their lives. What better way to honor myself and my experience but to teach others how I healed and what I learned in the process?

The next day I gave my two weeks notice to my employer and began the journey of Chris Sopa International. Has everything been perfect along the way? NO! Did everything turn out exactly as I expected it to? NO! But here is the thing: I knew if I never tried it that I would never know. It is always better to try and "fail" than it is to not try at all and wonder your whole life, "I wonder what my life would have been like if....?"

When I found out my Dad was terminally ill, I promised myself that I would not allow him to die with the thought in my head of "I wish I would have..." To me, that would have been worse than his death. The thought of knowing that I could have done something, could have spent more time with him, could have told him I loved him...and didn't. That came down to purely my choice.

I now live my life with my "unwilling to do list" empty. My friend Donna and I are "bucket list buddies." We each have a bucket list of things we want to accomplish and do before we die and we take it very seriously. We are affectionately known as "Thelma and Louise" to all of our friends... mainly because when we go someplace together, we're traveling in Donna's 1966 red convertible Mustang! There is nothing on either of our lists we are unwilling to at least try. We both decided, after major events in our lives, to stop living our life based on our fears and start living our life based on our dreams. There is a HUGE difference! Living your life based on your dreams takes courage: courage to face what you fear (such as when I went skydiving to face my extreme fear of heights!) instead of running from it and avoiding it. Courage isn't the absence of fear, it is doing what you fear *in spite* of the fear. When you accomplish something you always thought you could never do, the feeling you are left with is one of pride, joy, and a strong realization that nothing in life is "that bad."

Taking a risk has to do with having faith that you are never alone and that there is a higher plan in order for you—a plan that supersedes your own plan that you can choose to walk if you wish. If everyone always took the "safe road," imagine what we would have never seen to bless our lives today: computers, cars, the Internet, video games, airplanes, cures for diseases, books, etc. Someone had to take a risk, in spite of everyone else's sniping that it "won't work" and that "you are crazy" to create those things.

I guess it all depends on how you look at the word "failure." If failure to you means something not working out as you thought it would, then you will live your life safe and feel disappointed most of your life. If failure to you means one step closer to what will work (such as Edison who took 1000 tries to come up with the idea for the light bulb!) then you will live your life full of experiences, all of which you will look at from the perspective of a positive learning experience. Your perception is your reality and your perception is your choice!

Sometimes we try so hard to make a certain outcome reality that we actually get in our own way. This intense effort comes from a place of fear of wanting a certain outcome that we think is for our best instead of a possible other outcome that may cause us pain. The more we try, the more we actually push the outcome we desire away. Since everything in the universe is made up of energy, everyone and everything can read energy. The energy of something is the attention you are putting on it. So if I really like someone and want to date them and think "that is the man for me" and my fear is that if he doesn't like me, someone else may not come around, then I am going *to try* to force the outcome I want on the situation. He feels the energy of me forcing that outcome and although he cannot put his finger on it, he just feels something is "not right."

Allowing yourself to relax into the bigger plan and divine timing is a risk. You are risking being hurt. You are risking an outcome you think is in your best interest, when in reality there may even be a better plan out there waiting for you. Your risk is in having faith that things will always work out "as intended." We constantly seek for the answers to our troubles "out there" when all along the answers to our troubles are "in here"—inside each of us, waiting to blossom. All we have to do is trust, take risks, and, instead of constantly looking outward, begin to inwardly seek the peace that awaits us.

MISTAKES

"If I had my life to live over…I'd dare to make more mistakes next time."
~Nadine Stair

Once you begin to understand that everything in life happens for a reason, you begin to view the idea of "mistakes" in a very different light. Was it really a mistake to date that person? Was it really a mistake to take that job? Was it really a mistake to go on that trip?

More than likely, if you would have not had those experiences you call "mistakes," you would not be the person you are today. You would not have the strength, the knowledge and the wisdom that makes up who you are.

We fear mistakes for many reasons, most of which are personal. Some people fear what others think, some fear failure again, and some fear rejection. The fears we have about mistakes come from our conditioning; what we were taught and what we saw as we were growing up is ingrained in the back of our minds. Sometimes what we fear didn't even happen to us but someone we knew and it was so impactful that it became our fear as well.

Many people view mistakes as something bad, something that should not have happened and made them feel a way in which they did not want to feel. If you made a choice that led you down a path you did not want, don't continue to relive it in your mind over and over again. Instead, begin to look at mistakes as opportunities to learn. Your only purpose here on earth is to grow. There are no accidents and there are no mistakes. A mistake is only a "mistake" if you did not learn and grow from it. When you fret over a mistake and keep re-playing it in your mind, you are only drawing the energy and vibration of that mistake to your present time, and nothing more. What you think about most you "bring about"; if you are thinking constantly about how you said or did the wrong thing, guess what you will "attract" to you? Guess what will happen again? You guessed right: that very same "mistake!"

Instead of dwelling on the negative, think about what you learned and take that with you and leave the experience behind. Stop dragging the entire experience with you to relive over and over again. Ask yourself, "What can I do differently in this situation next time?" Then, the next time you are presented with a situation that is similar, you can pause, remember your "mistake" from the last time, and make a different choice. Mistakes are proof that you are trying and moving forward!

One of the hardest things to do after we have made a mistake is to forgive ourselves. I only recently discovered why...

One of my personal struggles, which I have battled for as long as I can remember, is wanting people to like me. This, of course, stems from having a fear about what other people think of you. I find this ironic since in the profession I chose—public speaking—I am constantly putting myself in the spotlight, sharing my personal stories, and allowing myself to be vulnerable and open to "attacks" of dislike! From the observer point of view, however, how better for me to learn this hard lesson than to put myself in situations time and time again where someone doesn't agree with or like me? What an awesome school! The good news is that I am aware of this limiting belief but sometimes the awareness doesn't necessarily make it "easy" to change—especially if it is one that has been ingrained in you for a very long time. That's why, even after I became an established speaker, I still struggled with the fear of not being liked. This was especially difficult in romantic relationships. If my significant other did not respond how I thought he should, or, God forbid, broke up with me, I immediately went to the place where I blamed myself and assumed it was something that I must have done or said to push him away. I would have the hardest time forgiving myself if I did find something I said or did that changed how he felt about me; in fact, I would relive it over and over again in my mind like a self-masochist!

It then finally occurred to me that in the realm of sacred contracts, we have had many people in our lives who are *scripted* to do some kind of "harm" to us, either emotionally, mentally, or sometimes physically; their "job," so-to-speak, is to cause us enough pain to see our lesson and hopefully learn and change from the situation. And it's just possible that *we* are are also scripted to play the role of the "villain" for others as well. Sometimes our "mistakes" needed to happen in order for us to play "the teacher" and help someone else learn a hard lesson.

When this epiphany hit me, it was as if a wave of forgiveness washed over me. I immediately saw some of my recent relationships in a new perspective, and realized that what I perceived I did "wrong" was ok. Even if those people (we're talking about all kinds of relationships now) may not choose to have me in their lives, even if they have a view of me that may not be accurate, even if I may never see them again, I played a part in their story. I hit the ball back into their court so they then could choose to learn one of the lessons they scripted to learn. Now THAT, my friends, is a spiritual partnership!

FORGIVING YOURSELF

"I know how long you've carried it around and how heavy it is.

Just let it go.

Deep down, you know it was just one of those things.

Just let it go.

You've had it for so long, it's hard to imagine life without it.

Just let it go.

You know we weren't made to hang on to it.

Just let it go.

Right now. This moment. You've waited long enough.

Just let it go.

Take all of that forgiveness locked up deep inside of you and...

Just let it go."

This is the hardest yet the most important part of this whole process of release. Forgiveness is a tricky thing. It is something we know we must do to finally let go so we can move on; yet, we hold on to hurt and blame because it somehow gives us a satisfaction we cannot explain. When we think about forgiveness, we immediately think about those outside of us we need to forgive; in actuality, the first place we need to begin is with ourselves. If you think it is hard to forgive someone else for something they may have done or said to you, try to forgive yourself! Our ego loves to harbor all of that resentment towards the self because it keeps us small. Beating ourselves up, feeling guilty, and being shamed around some wrong we did keeps us in a downward spiral and gives us a permanent excuse not to "step it up" in life. After all, what happens if we make another mistake and do something else wrong? Then we will feel even worse; so why bother. If you keep living in the fear of making the mistake again, what a wonderful excuse not to take risks, hold yourself accountable, and try new things. Perfect!

"Once we have forgiven ourselves for something, it is easier to forgive others for the same mistake."
~Marianne Williamson

Remember that how we treat others is merely a reflection of how we treat ourselves. If you have a hard time letting go of mistakes you have made, more than likely you have a hard time letting go of mistakes others have made as well. The only way to really find peace is to let the past be the past. Keep it where it belongs. Your subconscious mind does not know the difference between what is real and what is not; it only knows on what you put your attention. If you are reliving a past moment in your head constantly, your subconscious mind thinks it is actually happening again! It doesn't know you are just "thinking" about it. It brings up all of the emotions as if it is happening again right now! Why would you want to relive pain and hurt? Let it go....

Self-forgiveness includes admitting to yourself that you are human. Humans are made to make mistakes because mistakes, as you remember, are how we learn. The moments where we make mistakes are the moments for which we came here. Those moments are our classroom. When you think of your life in this way, there is really nothing to forgive. We cannot make a "wrong" choice as long as that choice has given you an opportunity to learn. Every moment is perfect as is. Put to bed the guilt and shame…those feelings do not come from God. Those feelings come from your lower self wanting to keep you down. If a feeling does not empower you to be better than you are, than you have no use for it. Get rid of it.

Be patient with yourself. Those old feelings will want to continue to creep up on you; that's where your boundaries and self-discipline come in. Don't be afraid to talk right to your feelings and say, "Excuse me, you have no place here. Go away!" You have to constantly monitor yourself and keep yourself in check. Be your own parent. Care enough about yourself to care where you allow your mind to go at every moment. Focus your attention on unconditional love for yourself and others.

In regards to forgiving others, Louise Hay, I think, states it the best:

"We are the ones who suffer when we hold on to past grievances. We give the situations and the people in our past power over us, and the same situations and people keep us mentally enslaved. They continue to control us when we stay stuck in "unforgiveness." This is why forgiveness work is so important. Forgiveness – letting go of the ones who hurt us – is letting go of our identity as the one who was hurt. It allows us to be set free from the needless cycle of pain, anger, and recrimination that keep us imprisoned in our own suffering. What we forgive is not the act, but the actors – we are forgiving their suffering, confusion, unskillfullness, desperation and their humanity. As we get the feelings out and let them go, we can then move on. Remember that all of the events that take place in our lives and all of the individuals we encounter teach us valuable lessons."

Forgiveness is a soul choice and centers in your heart. It is not a logical, mental process. It has nothing to do with whether or not you choose to have that person stay in your life or not. You can forgive someone and choose to not have them in your life anymore or choose to have them stay ... it is up to you. Every choice you make must be for your own peace. Never sacrifice your inner peace for someone else. Forgiveness is an act of self-love and healing. The reason for forgiving someone is not so much because you feel they deserve to be forgiven, but because you love yourself enough to not want to suffer anymore when you think about the person or the event. We learn to suffer just to punish whoever abused us and, in the end, we are the only ones who are hurt.

You know forgiveness has occurred the same way you know a wound has healed. When a wound has healed you can touch it and it doesn't hurt anymore. When you have forgiven someone, you can think of that person or the event that took place and there is no longer an emotional charge around it. The pain is gone.

Never forget that each of us is on our own journey. We choose to play roles for each other to give each other an opportunity to learn the life lessons we came here to learn. Thank the people who have hurt you for playing their roles so well. If it wasn't for those who have hurt us the most, we would not be the people we are today.

Life is about balance. As energy beings, we are constantly trying to find this balance through relationships, jobs, conversations, or experiences. Each experience we have that brings us closer to balance, such as forgiveness, raises our spiritual vibration; or, to put it another way, gets us closer to God.

WHAT YOU DO AND THINK AFFECTS OTHERS

Many of you might make decisions based on fear because you do not believe the outcome "you" think is best for you will appear. But, the key word here is *you*. Sometimes what we think is best for us is not really in our highest good. Sometimes there is another path that may not look as obvious but will get us to the same destination. Remember, God has a much higher perspective than we do. He can see into our hearts and minds as well as into those of others. He truly can see what the "highest path" for us can be…we just have to have faith in what we scripted for ourselves in this lifetime to learn. Highest good means what is best for all, not just you! We are all one, and our lives are all intermingled. Whatever you think or do affects everyone!

One day on a bus coming home from a Chamber of Commerce function, I had the distinct pleasure of sitting next to a man who told me an amazing story. I was drawn to go to this event, an event I would have never chosen myself to go to, for a specific reason. Although I did not know what that reason was when I signed up to go, I went anyway. Sometimes in life you just have to "show up." This man, let's call him Al, told me of a time in his life where he had a very serious accident and actually had an out-of-body experience before waking up in the midst of being resuscitated in the emergency room. He was coming home from an out-of-town trip late at night and pulled over to the side of the road to check a map because he was lost. In this brief moment, his car was hit by a semi-trailer that swerved off the road. The next thing he knew, he found himself floating above his car looking down at himself. He then went on to describe how two angels appeared on either side of him and a feeling like a vacuum pulling him backwards jolted him through a white tunnel. He ended up in a white room with two doors. He was guided to a chair in the middle of the room and took a seat. Through the door in front of him appeared the most peaceful and loving figure he had ever seen. He said the unconditional love coming from this being, who he felt was Jesus, made him immediately fall to his knees and weep. This figure placed his hand on Al's head and said, "My son, it is not your time. You have more to do. Before we send you back, someone would like to speak to you."

At this moment, the figure disappeared and the other door opened. Through the open door came Al's grandmother who had passed away a year earlier. She asked him to take a ride with her. She then proceeded to take Al to different scenes in his life to show him how his actions and his thoughts affected others. The interesting part about this part of the journey was that Al actually experienced what *the other person* felt during the scene he was being shown...he was in "their shoes" this time. You see, up to this point, Al had not lived a life of which he was proud. He worked many hours, was a regular at strip clubs, and lived a life of cheating on his wife and lying. Not something he was proud of discussing. After seeing how his choices affected others in ways he never imagined, his grandmother took him to a bridge where they were surrounded by water.

She held out her hand which was closed around an object and held it over the body of water. When she opened her hand, she showed Al a small pebble in the middle of her palm. Turning her hand over, the pebble hit the water as he watched a ripple go through the entire body of water. His grandmother then turned to him and said, "Never forget that everything you *do* and *think* affects everyone else. Just like this one small pebble affected this entire body of water. One person CAN make a difference. We are all connected. Now go and make different choices."

Al then described a feeling of being jolted backwards and the next thing he knew he was being defibrillated in the emergency room. He described going back into his body like putting on a glove that was too small. He had broken almost every bone in his body due to the impact of the truck and spent nine months in rehab—enough time for him to think about how he was going to change his life. He quit his job and started over, not knowing if it would work out but knowing he had to make a different choice.

When Al was finished telling me his story, we both wiped our tears and he looked at me and said, "The only other person who knows that story is my wife. I have no idea why I just told you that." I then realized why I was supposed to go to that event...

We cannot do anything without it affecting someone else. When you pray for the highest good in any situation, you pray for not just what is best for you, but what is best for all. Al had to have hope that his new choices would bring him the life he desired, for himself and his family. He had to have faith that no matter what he chose, God had his back.

THE PURPOSE OF PAIN

"Until the pain of staying the same is greater than the pain of changing, you will stay the same."

Pain. It is something we all go to extreme measures to avoid. We will sacrifice obvious experiences that would bring us happiness simply due to the mere chance we may experience pain. Pain is many things, but most of all, it is the greatest blessing we have.

Let's consider for a minute the purpose of physical pain. When you touch a hot stove, you experience pain and pull your hand away. The pain told you to pull your hand away because the stove was hurting you. If it wasn't for the pain, you would keep your hand there, burn it and more than likely have no skin left after a few minutes! The pain was your signal saying, "Hey, this is not good for you!"

Now let's put this in perspective of your emotions. The pain you suffer emotionally acts in the same way. It is a signal letting you know that this "thing" making you feel bad needs to be looked at a little closer. Emotional pain comes in the form of frustration, doubt, heart-break, worry, blame, anger, hatred, jealousy, etc. Any one of these feelings is telling you that you are not in alignment with what you truly want, and who you truly *are* for that matter! Later we will discuss ways in which you can align yourself, but for now, know that pain in the form of "bad" emotions is your red flag that something needs to change.

Emotions are the language of the universe and the most powerful part of this language is that which gets our attention. When we are living in fear, we are deaf, blind, and dumb. When you are afraid of something, what happens? You cannot think, you are not clear, your senses begin to focus only on that thing you fear, and you hear and see nothing else around you. You have tunnel vision around your fear because you are afraid it will come true and are afraid of feeling pain.

When I was suffering from my colitis, I was terrified. Being a control freak as I was, it was the first time in my life I could not control something that was happening to me. Taking an antibiotic for 7-10 days while I still chugged away at work was not going to cure this one! I was terrified because I was in new territory—the territory of the unknown. I had no clue how to heal myself or deal with my situation. So I kept myself busy. Very busy. Being busy is the absolute best excuse for avoiding what you know one day you are going to have to face. "I cannot deal with the fact that my marriage is failing right now...I am too busy. I will wait until work slows down and the kids graduate." It's the perfect excuse: Who is going to argue with you if they see you running around like a maniac, driving yourself and everyone around you crazy in the process? They couldn't catch you anyway! Avoidance, however, can only last so long...

As I was healing myself, I realized that if I had not become sick, I would never have slowed down enough on my own to change. I didn't know how. I began to look at my illness as a blessing in disguise. After all, if I had never gotten sick, I wouldn't even be writing this book you are now reading! Pain is a gift with its own purpose because you are never going to grow if everything is perfect all of the time. The only way to live life from a higher level is to release the negativity and unfinished business from your life. Remember:

"Until the pain of staying the same is greater than the pain of changing, you will stay the same."

Everything that happens in your life happens for a reason: every person you meet, every painful event, every happy event, everything! Everything you experience is a chance for you to get closer to God—a chance to learn something new about yourself and how you function in the world around you. Learn to see pain as a blessing – a red flag showing you where you need to change or release something you no longer need in your life. Engage the lessons life is trying to teach you. Look at your life ... where is the pain and what is it asking you to look at or change?

"Sometimes is it that which shatters us that liberates us."
~ Marianne Williamson

Iain Petrie was leaving a pub one evening and got mugged by four men, leaving him bleeding on the street with a knife wound to the leg and a broken cheekbone. Upon arriving at the hospital, a scan of his head revealed more than just a broken cheek bone..Iain had a brain tumor! Iain had no symptoms of a brain tumor before the mugging and most likely may not have known about it until it was too late. You could say the mugging, an event most would look at as a negative, was a blessing in disguise.

The most beautiful part of pain is that when you learn your lesson, the pain goes away. The worst part is that if you choose not to learn the lesson when the pain arrives, it will come back. And because you did not listen the first time, the pain increases each go around…and keeps increasing until you finally learn the lesson. How else can your attention be grabbed if not through pain? Think about the greatest lessons you have learned in your life so far—the ones that have stuck with you and changed you forever. I'm willing to bet you suffered some kind of pain to learn that lesson so hard.

When I am feeling any kind of pain in my life, I have found that it usually means I am being tested, or that some major transformation or positive change is around the corner; the painful event acts as a "clearinghouse" to get rid of the old, stagnant energies that are blocking the new energy's path into my life. When I find myself in the middle of one of these significant events, the feelings are always the same: I feel overwhelmed, unable to focus, very alone, unable to connect with my gifts. I cry a lot. I think every time, "God, why have you abandoned me!" This is why the poem, "Footprints" is hanging in my kitchen.

One night a man had a dream. He dreamed he was walking along the beach with the Lord.

Across the sky flashed scenes from his life. For each scene, he noticed two sets of footprints in the sand; one belonged to him and the other to the Lord.

When the last scene of his life flashed before him, he looked back at the footprints in the sand.

He noticed that many times along the path of his life there was only one set of footprints. He also noticed that it happened to be at the very lowest and saddest times of his life.

This really bothered him and he questioned the Lord about it. "Lord, you said that once I decided to follow you, you'd walk with me all the way. But I have noticed that during the most troublesome times in my life, there is only one set of footprints. I don't understand why when I needed you most you would leave me."

The Lord replied, "My precious, precious child, I love you and I would never leave you.

During your times of trial and suffering, when you only see one set of footprints, it was then that I carried you."

Every time I read that poem, it reminds me that I am never alone when I am going through pain. It reminds me that in order to appreciate what is good in my life, I have to experience the polar opposite: bad. The things that we term as "bad" or that cause us pain help us see those ordinary things in our life that are blessings…blessings that we have been ignoring day in and day out.

Surrender to what is. Be where you are in mind, body and spirit and say *yes* to life—pain and all! Then, life will work for you and not against you. It is always much easier to go *with* the flow of energy than *against* it. Remember, no matter how bad life seems today, we always get a second chance tomorrow.

When pain comes up, it usually means something is trying to be released. It could be an old limiting belief that has finally worn out or an emotion you have been pushing down for too long. When you release anything, you have in essence experienced a loss. We typically think of grieving only when someone we loved or cared about passes away, but grieving happens no matter what you have lost: a person, a job, a relationship, and even a habit. You've experienced a loss even when you move, have a lifestyle change, overcome a health issue of any kind—or when you let go of a limiting belief. This limiting belief you have has created habits of thought and behaviors that you may have had your whole darn life! Finally taking back your power and creating a new habit of thought and behavior is cause for celebration.

FAITH AND HOPE

"Faith is exactly what it takes to get through uncertainty. Faith is not necessary when you know how things are going to work out—that's knowledge. It's in the time of unknowing that having faith is what sees you through to the other side. Faith is what gives you strength. Faith is that light in your heart that keeps on shining even when it's all darkness outside. Now is the time to keep that faith alive!"

I often find myself wondering about the difference between faith and hope? Both require confidence, trust and belief in something or someone. Why two words when they seem to be the same thing? According to the definition of faith in Websters dictionary, faith requires a*"belief that does not rest on logical proof or material evidence."* Isn't "proof" what our society thrives on? Lawyers need proof, lovers need proof, scientists need proof, and God-seekers need proof. Proof is the basis for which we determine if something is "real." If I can touch it, smell it, and see it...then it is real. What I have found over the last several years in my life is that the things that are most "real" to me cannot be proven or touched, but sensed from a deeper part of my being. The things that change my life and turn it upside down (in good and bad ways!) are those things that were unpredicted and illogical at first—things that seemed surreal.

Faith is that unwavering belief that "it will be fine and work out for the highest good." This is very different than the attitude of "it will work out how *I want it to work out*!" When we can accept that there is a higher plan that supersedes ours and that sometimes we have volunteered ourselves to be "used" to teach someone else, or better yet ourselves, a lesson, then we are truly free from fear. We tend to get stuck on a certain outcome and then when it doesn't go exactly how we thought it should, we say "See, I knew it – God wasn't listening" or "things never go my way!" The victim role is never attractive! What we fail to have here is faith in that maybe, just maybe, *our* plan wasn't the best plan. Maybe *our* plan wasn't for the highest good.

Hope is the fuel that drives faith. Having grown up in a household where every serious conversation I had with my father ended with, *"Remember Chris, there is always hope,"* I always made the assumption I knew what hope was. It wasn't until my father was diagnosed with terminal cancer that I actually started to question my definition. Here was a man, dying and in pain, who still said he had hope. I remember feeling angry. Angry at God and angry at my father for holding out, what I called, "false hope." How could you possibly have hope when you already knew the outcome would be a grave one and one you did not want?

And then, suddenly, I realized: We never know the outcome, even if it looks like a slam dunk. At any moment, a miracle can occur. Our lives can shift and never be the same again. We were put on this Earth, in this life, as creators. We go through life not realizing that we manifest with our thoughts and beliefs as we trudge through every day. This is not a journey of discovery, it is a journey of creation. Our hopes *creates* the path we chose to walk on towards our desires.

"Hope is like a road in a country; there wasn't ever a road, but when many people walk on it, the road comes into existence."
~ Lin Yutang

I came to the realization that faith is that undying belief that no matter what, things will work out. That what we hope for will come true. We may not know how and we may not know when, but we know in every fiber of our being, in the soul of our souls, the best thing possible for us will manifest. Faith is trusting in your divine spiritual contract. Our higher self scripted certain events to help us move forward toward the next dimension of being. We knew before we came into this world what we needed to learn to take that leap, once and for all, to the next level of our soul. Faith is the string that attaches our physical being to that manifest part of our soul. It is the lifeline that allows the light within to shine so bright that the possibility of something happening other than what is for our highest good is impossible. It is the peace that manifests in every fiber of our being because it knows that we are never alone, that we are always protected, and there is nothing that can manifest in our lives that we cannot handle.

"Faith is the invisible security in a world of visible chaos."

I like to think of hope as the light that shines the way for faith to take hold.

Hope makes it possible for faith to exist. Faith is being sure of what we hope for and certain of what we do not see.

CHAPTER SEVEN

LISTENING TO CLUES

"Your daily life is your temple and your religion. Whenever you enter into it, take with you your all."
~Kahil Gibran, "The Prophet"

We all have spirit guides, or some may like to call them "guardian angels." Our guides live in the spirit world and their role is to guide us along the path we have chosen to follow. They were there with us before our birth when we scripted our contract. They remember the discussion that was had so they give us little nudges, so to speak, every once and a while to help us remember what we wanted to accomplish while we were here this time. They speak to us in different ways; through our dreams, feelings, other people, coincidences, and sometimes even directly if you are in tune with your spiritual gifts.

My friend Elaine and I have always been the type of friends that can tell each other anything…and we trust each other implicitly. We have become very open and very good (I must say) at "listening" to what our guides and the Universe are trying to tell us.

One night, after Elaine and I went to dinner, we ended up back at her house for our usual cup of tea and reading of oracle cards. The previous few weeks, I had been clearing and releasing some *major* karmic debris and old patterns around romantic relationships, culminating in a renewed outlook on how I was "being" in my relationships with men and realizing the strange connection it had to the relationship with my parents. Toward the end of the night, I received a phone call from an old flame who wanted to take me out at the last minute to a movie. I graciously accepted, thinking it wouldn't hurt to see him since we were "friends." I said my good-byes to Elaine and got into my cute little red VW Beetle (whom I affectionately call "Lucy"), started my car, and began to back up. After going about 2 inches, my car started to move forward instead of backwards. I assumed I did not have it all the way in gear, put it back in gear and tried again...this time not moving backwards at all and only moving forward. At this point, I'm panicked because I knew that I did not have money for a new transmission, which was apparently the problem. I got out of my car and knocked on Elaine's door again. When she answered I said, "My car won't go backwards!" She looked right at me and said, "Ok, you need to come inside." She proceeded to tell me that at the precise moment I said "My car won't go backwards" she heard from my guides, "She is not allowed to go backwards!" Being the honest friend that she is, she told me she did not think I was supposed to go out that night with my old flame for some reason. After calming me down, we sat down and consulted our guides about the matter. Through oracle cards and our own intuitions, they proceeded to tell me that I had made great progress in clearing out un-needed energies from my energy field and going out that night with this old flame would be the equivalent of moving backwards and it would have dire consequences to the advancement I had made thus far.

Sometimes, our guides use the material things (and people) in our lives to get us messages as well as to protect us from going down a path they know may not be good for us. Of course, we always have free will. I could have said, screw the car, borrowed my friend's car and gone out with my ex anyway. But, I decided to heed the clues I was getting—since they went to so much trouble to get me the message in the first place, I felt it was the least I could do! Our guides are brilliant in knowing how to best draw our attention to a topic. Although my car did indeed end up with a mechanical problem, the whole situation drew my attention to a pattern they did not want me to repeat.

The following morning, I was guided through a dream to repeat the phrase, "I am worth being loved unconditionally" over and over again until this pattern was "reframed" in my subconscious. The limiting belief I had been telling myself in relationships all of these years was that I needed to *do* something in order for someone to love me because I did not feel "just being me" was enough. After reframing this belief by usings affirmations and a technique I learned that uses muscle testing to see what the *true* beliefs are of your subconscious mind, my guides guided me through a meditation where my deceased father, deceased grandmother, Jesus, Mary Magdalene, and Archangel Michael all assisted.

Being able to "hear" the clues that are being sent our way consists of not only staying in present time but also learning to look at your life from more of an "observer" role, as we have mentioned before, rather than a "player" role. When we are an observer, we are detached from the emotions of the situation and can truly see the symbology involved. We tend to look at challenges in our life not as obstacles but as learning tools. Every encounter and every situation is a vehicle to help us learn something to move to the next level of awareness. We see the world from a bigger perspective: one that includes what is best for "the whole," not just what is best for "us as an individual." It gives us a chance to stop and ask, "What is *really* going on here?"

The player only ever sees things literally and tends to analyze the situation using the mind and reason. Where heaven is concerned, there is no logic. Some things just don't "make sense" to our brains but make perfect sense to heaven. Remember, we have a very limited perspective from "down here." The heavens see all that is, in all directions of time. Personally, I trust their guidance more than my own. All we need to do is keep our eyes…and ears…open.

On the last day of my father's funeral, as were saying our good-byes to family and friends, the funeral home director approached us. In her hand she carried a stack of booklets regarding how to deal with the loss of a loved one. I took the booklets and looked down at them briefly. Something told me to look again and that's when I noticed the author of all those booklets: Father Herb Weber. Father Herb was the priest who was the pastor of the church I went to in college; the priest I traveled to Mexico with in my sophomore year in college to learn about the culture and beliefs there; the priest who baptized both of my daughters; the priest whom I turned to for years when I needed higher wisdom of a spiritual nature: in short, the priest who was always there for me. His words comforted me back then in a way you just cannot explain. He always said the right thing and it was always exactly what I needed to hear. And in my hand, in that funeral home, there were his words comforting me again in a time when I probably needed them most. Coincidence? I don't think so.

COMFORT

When we are going through trying times and fear is pervading our every thought, comfort comes in many forms. All we have to do is be present and *listen*. We are never, ever alone on our journey. There are no coincidences. We forget as humans that we have other senses beyond the five that we know: psychic senses of vision, auditory, intuition and kinesthetic as well as our sleeping dreams. We need to learn to tap into these senses more than ever when we are facing challenges in our lives. It is through these channels that we get our most important messages. These are the channels through which our deceased loved ones whom we miss so dearly live on. These are the channels through which our spirit guides and angels speak to us. All we have to do is be open, be present, and listen.

WHERE IS YOUR ATTENTION

Where your thoughts go, energy flows. I want to expand on that phrase for a moment to make it simpler to understand because this is probably the most important tool in your toolbox for developing yourself and moving beyond fear. If you recall, your subconscious mind works very differently from your conscious mind. Your subconscious mind has no filter. It believes what it gets from the conscious mind. The conscious mind is the place where you make your choices. You choose to accept or reject whatever information comes into your brain. Whatever choice you make filters down into the subconscious mind and that is what it acts on.

What you may not realize is that it is more than the thought: It is where you are putting your attention. Attention is thought mixed with a feeling. Your thought is like the car and the feeling is like the gas. Your car goes nowhere fast without gas in it. A thought goes nowhere without a feeling attached to it and every thought conjures up a feeling—usually grabbing an old feeling to which it is attached from a past event in your life (conditioning) which may or may not serve you at this time.

The most important self-discipline you can master is that of monitoring your attention. The minute you find yourself "feeling bad" you need to immediately stop what you are doing and ask yourself, "Where is my attention?" Is it on something you want in your life or something you don't want? That attention acts as implicit instructions to the universe to act! Stop what you are doing, say to yourself, "Cancel, clear, and delete!" and direct your attention to what you want to manifest instead. This takes practice, patience, and work. It is not easy at first but the more you do it the more it becomes a habit—and you will soon realize you don't like "feeling bad" and will immediately begin to direct your attention to the things that make you feel better.

Pay attention to the words you speak as well. My good friend, Chris Whitcoe of Pure Joy Academy, calls this *conscious languaging*. The words we choose to speak create our reality because they elicit feelings and direct our attention to that thing of which we are speaking. Monitor your language and word choice as a discipline and pay attention to the intention you give each thought and each word. Whatever you put out into the universe, the universe always responds in kind.

LISTEN TO YOUR BODY

When asked what surprises him the most, the Dalai Lama answered: "Man, because he sacrifices his health in order to make money. Then he sacrifices money to recuperate his health. And then he is so anxious about the future that he does not enjoy the present; the result being that he does not live in the present or the future; he lives as if he is never going to die, and then he dies having never really lived."

Once you begin to love yourself, you realize that your "self" talks to you all of the time. It tells you what you need and what is best for you. The main way our higher self talks to us is through our physical body. We are 3D beings on a 3D planet and one of our main roles is to learn how to be in a 3D reality (which includes our physical bodies, emotions, logic, etc.), yet at the same time use our 4D abilities (intuition, clairvoyance, etc.). If you have been paying attention throughout this book, you have seen how much what you hold in your mind influences the world around you. What you hold in your mind also affects your physical body. I have always said that when God wants to get your attention he hits you physically – that is the only way that will stop us sometimes. Why? Because we are conditioned to plow through the physical, taking for granted that our health will always be there. Ask yourself this question: If your child or someone you love had a headache, what would you tell them to do? More than likely you would tell them they needed to rest, to lay down, drink some water, take a bath, get something to eat, etc. Now, what do *you* do when you have a headache? That's right…you take a pill! Admit it! The last thing you do is "slow down." It is forbidden! I mean, you have important things to do that if they don't get done someone will surely die…right?

The best thing you can do is to learn to listen to your body signals so you can catch them and interpret them before they turn into a physical crisis. Our bodies have their own unique language and they tell us what we need, every time! Begin to recognize where in your body you feel "stress" and when. I know for me personally I have different types of headaches. I have a tired headache, a hungry headache, an "I'm getting sick" headache, etc. I have learned the difference by paying attention to my physical body and putting the pieces together when I become aware of them. You see, because we are so "busy" and "rushed" all of the time, we are not present and when we are not present there is no way we can be aware of what we are holding in our physical bodies. We have dense, physical bodies in this 3D reality for a reason. Since we have a veil that is keeping us from knowing the truth—that we ourselves are Divine—our physical-ness acts as a communication vessel. It tells us what is going on with us mentally, emotionally, and spiritually. The physical is the last place an "issue" manifests. Your feelings are even a physical embodiment of the Divine's guidance to you. You feel your feelings physically just as you do if you cut your finger—both being a sign that "this thing here needs paying attention to!"

Every year I take a small group on a journey to Peru where we spend 12 days in this sacred country hiking the Inca trail and visiting Machu Picchu, the Sacred Valley and the Amazon jungle. This is not a vacation; this is a spiritual journey. My participants are challenged mentally, physically, emotionally and spiritually. One of the biggest lessons they learn while hiking the Inca trail is to listen to their bodies and how to give it what it needs. They experience things from altitude sickness to twisted ankles, all signs their body is sending them because it is "out of balance." They must learn what is needed to bring their bodies back into balance. As we hike, we learn that the spiritual body actually holds the physical body. We have all seen this to be true when we witness an amazing physical feat by somebody that we know is physically impossible. It's like the bumblebee: Based on its physical body, it is impossible that it should be able to fly, but it does. Why? Because its physical body doesn't know better; it is taking direction from its spiritual and mental self. When you hold something strongly in your mind, the physical simply becomes a vehicle to assist you in making it happen. It is never an obstacle. Whether you believe you can do a thing or not, you are right.

INTENTIONS

*"It is conscious **intention** which confers potency in the life
of each disciple and initiate."*
~ Djwhal Khul, the Tibetan

Our intentions are more powerful than we think they are. We have
discussed a lot here about the power of what we hold in our minds on
a daily basis and how that affects your reality. You may be thinking
about what is or what happened—or you may be thinking about what
you *intend* to do in the future.

Intention, as defined by Marilyn Schlitz of the Institute of Noetic
Sciences, is *"the projection of awareness, with purpose and efficacy, toward
some object or outcome."* The power of an intention spans beyond what
we have been taught. Schlitz conducted intensive research in the psychic
community on DMILS (Direct Mental Interaction with Living Systems),
which is defined as the ability of human thought to influence the world
around it. She conducted several experiments connecting how one
person's thoughts can influence another through the electrical signaling
in the brains of the people involved. Schlitz also describes thought and
intention much like a star. A star radiates out like starlight and affects
everything in its path. When we focus our thoughts on one thing in
particular, or hold an intention for something, we are directing all of
our energy towards that one thing. That one thing then feels the signal
we are sending it and via the law of attraction, pulls it toward us. That
is how powerful intention is!

I was with a coaching client the other day and we were sitting
there discussing her ex-husband's wife, of whom she is not fond, and
a situation she had just encountered with her. We started to joke that
it would be so much fun if we had a button we could push to "reset" a
situation after it occurs. That way, you could say what you want and do
what you want to the person, hit "reset" *and then* do the "right" thing.
(I know…that doesn't sound very nice, does it?) This way, you feel the
satisfaction of having said what was on your mind but no one would
remember it. Of course, we were joking, but as we were discussing

this, a voice popped into my head revealing to me that no matter what the action ends up being, the intention is always recorded—therefore, squishing our button theory! Because intention is what you are holding in your heart, anything in your heart is recorded. Our heart is where our intentions are born.

When we can ultimately learn to focus our intentions on only those things that are of the highest good and the highest good of all, our life takes a turn in a direction that is the equivalent of living a miracle every day. You begin to manifest things almost immediately! You begin to see that all events in your life are synchronistic and happen for a reason. You begin to see that the events and people in your life are there to teach you and show you things about yourself that you need to learn, release or heal. Living a life such as this is called "living a life from your heart." You are truly heart-centered in everything you do, every decision you make and every intention you hold within your heart. Life becomes easy, joyful, and flows naturally in the direction of your highest good—as was always intended.

"The head is the surface level of thinking; the heart is the depth."
~*"Love is a Choice," Hemfelt, Minirth and Meier*

DIVINE TIMING

The most important lesson we can learn is that of Divine timing. Human nature is to want what we want, when we want it. We cannot understand why we cannot have what we want, how we want it, NOW! The fact of the matter is, and brace yourself, there is a higher agenda than the one you have created in your head....YOU ARE NOT IN CONTROL! You are here living your life in an illusion – behind a veil. That veil is the lie with which we were born that tells us we are not Divine, that we are sinners and somehow not worthy. That veil is now being lifted. More and more people are becoming enlightened to the truth; the truth that you are Divine and have God *within you*. We are all pieces of the Divine living out our lives together; as One. The illusion is that we are separate from each other—individuals. The truth is that what any one person does affects the whole. (Remember the pebble in the ocean from the story with Al?). It has always been that way and always will be. If one cell of your body goes bad it sends a message to the other cells of your body and they go bad; that is called dis-ease. Any dis-ease is simply your body being out of balance. It is impossible to be out of balance if you are in a state of joy in the present moment.

Take the time to breathe in your life. Know you are here for a divine purpose. Stop wasting time just coasting through your life. Define what you want and go get it! A brilliant coach I had once said to me: *"Instead of waiting for your ship to come in, swim out to the damn ship!"* Know from the moment you wake up what you want to "swim too" that day. Take the time to enjoy the things that you have defined that are important to you. Those are the things that really matter and you will soon realize that when you focus on those important things, everything else comes to you effortlessly.

"Slow down and everything you are chasing will come around and catch you."
~John De Paola

You will soon realize that the moment you have been waiting for does not require waiting and the things that you remember most will not be *things* at all. You can't control the length of your life; but you can control the depth.

CHAPTER EIGHT

YOUR HIDDEN GIFTS

"There is no better way to bring one to a knowledge
of himself than to lead him to a knowledge of the powers
that are lying dormant within his own soul."
~ Ralph Waldo Trine

We are all very aware of our five senses: touch, taste, hearing, vision, and smell. What many are unaware of is that we actually have four psychic senses as well: visual, auditory, intuition, and kinesthetic. Everyone has these. They are senses just like your 3rd dimensional, very familiar five senses, but they take a little more work to tap into due to the fact that when you use them you are actually tapping into 4th dimensional abilities. The fourth dimension is beyond the veil. It is another dimension in time that is our next stop after the physical life we are experiencing now. The fourth dimension is where our loved ones who have crossed over are "hanging out." It looks just like the third dimension, but with a more opaque characteristic. When you tap into these 4th dimension abilities, you can actually "see" your loved ones. The last scene in the movie "Ghost" with Patrick Swayze and Demi Moore actually represents what a spirit looks like in fourth dimension fairly accurately. It looks and feels like our third dimension world, but there are different "rules."

Part of our "job" while we are hanging out in this third dimension reality having a human experience is to learn how to experience God while we are here. Edgar Cayce defines a *mystic* as someone who makes the transition from searching for God to spiritually experiencing God. If you were drawn to read this book, more than likely you are a "mystic in disguise." We often think of mystics in the form of priests, monks, bishops, etc. Although mystics can take that form, a true mystic is one on an active search to experience the Oneness of all that is. Mystics can also be teachers, healers, garbage men, lawyers, etc. It is not what you do, *it is who you are.* It is not what life situations you are presented with that define you but *how you respond* to those situations. This is your *response-ability.*

Our gifts show up in many ways and they are unique for each individual. The key is to trust what comes up for you. Don't second guess it, don't try to logic it…just trust it. Even if it makes no sense to you. The more you trust your gifts, the easier it is to use them on a daily basis.

INTUITION

Intuition is that sense that we all have of "just knowing" something and not really knowing how we know. Mothers understand this sense well. We have all heard of "mother's intuition." Mothers just seem to know when their child is sick, or when they are about to wake up in the middle of the night . Some call intuition a sixth sense or a gut feeling. Whatever you call it, you have it. Many people ask me how you know the difference between an accurate intuitive hit and a misleading or biased thought. The way I have always been able to tell is by how I feel when the hit comes to me. If I get a tingly sensation down my spine and I feel content, it is an intuitive hit. If it comes to me more than once (especially 3 or more times!), it is an intuitive hit. If I feel worried and keep going over and over it in my mind, it is probably a self-contrived thought. Always run whatever information you get through your heart, not your head. Remember, from the dimension which intuition comes, there is no right or wrong. If you get a hit, it must be for you and meant for you to use in some way. When we try to figure out a future idea with our present minds, it never works. We must stay heart-centered, have faith, and allow the hit we receive to mold and form on its own as we continue to listen and follow our guidance daily. Moses, my master spirit guide, tells me all of the time that I am on a "need to know" basis. I will only get what information I need at the present moment. If I get anymore than that, it may affect the choices I make for my future.

I found out my Dad had passed away in the Cusco airport in Peru on the day I was headed back to the States. I remember the turmoil I went through before I left on my three-week journey to Peru, contemplating over and over again if it was a good idea that I even go on the trip. I even spoke to my Dad about it. His response was, "Chris, something tells me that you have to go." This was one of those times where your spirit is guiding you to do something that is completely illogical to your reasoning mind. Those are the intuitive "hits" that you must never ignore. Logically, it made no sense at all to go away for three weeks when my dad was dying. All of the old guilty thoughts came rushing in when I would think about it: "I must be a bad daughter for even thinking about going out of the country when my Dad is dying!" "What if something happens and no one can get a hold of me?" "What will other people think of me that I am going on a trip when my Dad is dying?'

My trip to Peru was truly a spiritual journey. I spent most of the time with Incan Shaman taking part in ancient Incan ceremonies such as the "*despacho.*" It was ceremonies such as this one that I believe helped my Dad finally "heal." In Peru, the prayers for my Dad turned from self-serving prayers to prayers for his highest good. I prayed for his healing, in whatever form it was that would serve him.

I spoke to him on the phone the week before he died. Another example of an intuitive "hit." I had called my mom to see how everything was going before I left for the Apu's (word for mountains in Quechua) for four days, secluded 16,800 feet up in the mountains. She told me he had been admitted to the hospice hospital and gave me the phone number. I hung up with my mom and put the number in my wallet, thinking I would be home in a week and I would talk to him then. I heard a voice in my head that said, "Call him now." I ignored it at first, and then I heard it again. Knowing better, I picked up the phone and called the number. The phone rang about eight times and I was just about to hang up and heard the voice in my head again say, "No, let it ring." So, I let it ring. Five rings later, my Dad picked up the phone. He sounded sicker than I had ever heard him but still had that certain joyfulness to his voice that some just never lose. The first thing out of his mouth was not about him, it was about me. He asked how my trip was going. I told him it was amazing and that I was spending most of my time doing healing work for him. He seemed at peace now that his time was approaching. We talked for a little bit longer and then I hung up. I knew that was the last time I would speak to my Dad. But, I also knew there was more healing work to do and for some reason I needed to be in Peru to do it. You see, my father and I had our closure. We had no unfinished business to take care of in this lifetime. We were at peace with our relationship so I did not need to be there. He wanted, and needed, to take his journey home alone. We can't take away people's lessons, or their experiences. There are some journeys for which we just have a solo seat.

My mother and brother, who had taken over my role of caregiver while I was in Peru, needed this time with him without me there as well. Me, being the "rescuer" of the family, always swooped in to "save the day," to take care of what needed to be taken care of during my Dad's illness. What I never realized until I was in Peru was how this was actually a disservice to my mother and brother. Although they were frightened at what was happening to my father, they needed the experience of caring for him without me around. It was part of their healing in the process of my father passing, without me being in the way.

I left for Peru on March 12th and returned on April 7th, the day my dad passed. It felt very close to how it must feel when you swallow a rock when I heard my husband's voice on the phone telling me he had passed about an hour ago. He did not pass while I was in the Apu's and could not get home. He waited, and passed on the day of my return. I could not have gotten home any quicker than on that day. He waited. He knew. I was not supposed to see him again before he died. I knew that. I also knew he was finally out of pain and at peace. This whole process was for him, not for me. It hit me in the airport that day. I gave him what he needed and I needed to be "non-local" to do it or I may not have had the strength to stay away.

Today, I talk to my dad every day. I can feel in the morning if I have been with him in my dreams. I feel his presence around my children. He is more with me now than he was when he was alive. He now has a different vantage point. He told me he passed when he did because he felt he could be of more help to me and others from "the other side." And he has been.

Trusting yourself is key and I cannot stress this enough. There were times on every mountain I have climbed and every hike I have been on that I have had to trust my body to know what to do and trust my intuitive hits to tell me where to go when the path was not clear. Imagine if we learned to do this daily, mountain or not? Imagine if we actually trusted ourselves to know what was best for us? Imagine: the potential we could tap into and the energy we would save!

VISUAL

The visual sense can take two forms: seeing spirit, geometric shapes, or colors outwardly through your physical eyes, or seeing images, not unlike fast clips from a movie, in the eye of your mind (your third eye). Many of us have experienced this already and are just unaware of it. Have there been times where you swore you saw something with your peripheral vision, out of the corner of your eye? Have you ever seen white light or colors around objects or people?

Psychic vision is one of the harder senses to develop but can be done with practice and trust. My vision comes in the form of movie clips in my mind. When I talk to people, I sometimes get a quick visual in my mind of a scene from their lives or an image of their aura colors. Outward vision happens for me as well. There is nothing freakier than waking up in the middle of the night to a spirit standing next to your bed waiting to tell you something! (You do get used to it after awhile!)

A few years ago I was in my kitchen making dinner. I went into the refrigerator to take out vegetables to make a salad and when I turned around there was a little girl standing in my kitchen. I was so startled that I dropped everything I was holding and then she disappeared. Why did she disappear? Because the minute we allow fear into our energy field, our vibration drops and we can no longer maintain the high vibration needed to see into the 4th dimension where the spirits exist.

A few months later, I found out this little girl was me from a past life. She showed up again one day with my father holding his hand. My father told me she came to remind me of something I needed to remember—something that would help me with a situation I was going through at the time.

KINESTHETIC

Kinesthetic is another word for "how you feel." Unlike intuition, which is when you "know" something, your kinesthetic sense shows up as a feeling—for example, you meet someone you have never met before and feel as if you really like them. Another example is walking into a room and feeling that something is not right. Your feelings are a guidepost that can help you and protect you.

Practice paying attention to how things make you feel: touch, taste, smell, temperature, different tingly sensations, etc. These are all of the ways the kinesthetic sense can show up. How certain people, places, situations, and even thoughts make you feel is also important.

I have used this sense several times to leave a certain location, to not get on a plane, to not take a certain road, to stay home and not go out. Just the other week I was walking out my front door to go to the gym for a quick swim. My younger daughter was home alone. As I walked off of my porch, I got a very strong doom-and-gloom feeling that I should not leave the house. I immediately trusted it, turned around, and went back inside. I never knew why I wasn't supposed to go anywhere that night, but I felt instantly better when I stepped in the house.

The same thing happened the following week when I kept getting a feeling over and over again that I should pull my car into the garage when I got home. I did not want to do this because it isn't easy to get my car in the garage, but I did it anyway, moaning and groaning the whole time. In the middle of the night, we had a wind storm and I woke up to find a huge tree branch in my driveway right where my car would have been parked!

Sometimes I am made privy to why I felt a certain way but many times I am not. I just trust what I get and follow it. My internal guidance to me is more real than any external reality I can experience.

AUDITORY

Auditory is what you hear but your psychic auditory sense is a bit different. You actually hear from inside your mind rather than with your ears. When your auditory sense starts to emerge, it often sounds as if you are overhearing a conversation going on in the other room but you cannot quite make out what they are saying. Sometimes, out of nowhere, you will hear someone call your name. This has always been a strong sense for me and is so real that I sometimes have a hard time telling the difference between if someone in the room is speaking to me or if I am hearing something with my auditory sense.

I remember when I was very young, probably about four years old, and *The Price is Right* was on TV. I was watching it and the characters on the television started to have a conversation with me. (Remember, I was four years old so this was how this sense presented itself to me so I would not be scared). I had a long conversation about my grandmother with them and remember excitedly running in to tell my mother about the conversation I had just had. She looked at me and told me it was just my imagination. Bubble busted!!

In spite of this, I continued to pay attention to this sense as I grew up. And although, I have to admit, it freaked me out sometimes, I rely on it now as one of my main forms of guidance.

With any of these four psychic senses, remember that they will present themselves to you in a unique way. Trust what comes up for you. The most important thing I want you to take away from this is to be aware that you have these senses. Pay attention to them. Seek out teachers you trust to help you develop these senses more fully.

As you begin to use these senses on a daily basis in your life, you will notice that these senses will get you through those times when when you experience pain, grief, or suffering. They will be the warm blanket that covers you with the knowledge that you are never alone as the storm passes through.

CHAPTER NINE

MASTERING YOUR EMOTIONS

ENERGY AND VIBRATION LEVELS

We are energy beings. Everything we are is energy. Energy, in essence, is the divine vibration of all things. It is of what all that God created is made up. It takes many forms and can be given or taken away, but one thing that it always does is try to balance itself. It is a constant, and simply changes form when needed: That is the law of conservation at work. Energy is what attracts us to or repels us away from certain situations or people. The energy doesn't "feel right" so we back off. The energy of that person "feels good" so we get to know them better.

Your own personal energy is your vibration level. Everyone vibrates at a different level depending on what stage of their spiritual development they find themselves. The more you follow your guidance and the further along you are in learning the lessons you scripted to learn in this lifetime, the higher your vibration. If one person has a higher vibration than another, it does not mean that person is "better" than the other person; it simply means they are further along on their journey.

When two individuals meet and they are like each other (the energy of that person feels good), they are "in-sync." Their vibration levels are close in proximity to each other. We are energized by these people, we learn from them, we look up to them and we enjoy spending time with them. Every so often, two individuals find themselves not in-sync anymore. This usually happens because one of the individual's vibration level either rose or fell, leaving the two individuals no longer in sync. They are no longer an "energy match." In this instance, the person whose vibration level is higher usually experiences one of many "symptoms," including becoming tired, annoyed, frustrated, angry, or irritated. This same sensation sometimes happens in large crowds. For instance, whenever I go to the mall with my daughters, I am absolutely exhausted when I come home. Why does this happen? Remember, energy is always trying to balance itself. When someone of a higher vibration is around someone of a lower vibration, the person who is vibrating lower cannot come "up the ladder" so to speak, so the person who is vibrating higher has to "come down." This is not the natural or preferred state for the higher vibrating being and can only be maintained for so long before the being wants to go back up to the higher state at which it is comfortable. The lower vibrating individual actually pulls energy from the higher vibrating individual (unconsciously), therefore making him/her feel tired, irritated, or annoyed.

I was at a conference a few years ago and met several ladies there who had much in common with myself. One of the ladies in particular kept telling me over and over again how much I reminded her of her daughter, with whom she was not currently getting along . We all decided to have lunch the following day. At lunch, when this woman arrived, I immediately began to feel tired, almost to the point of falling asleep at the lunch table! I remember feeling frustrated that I was having a hard time staying awake and chalked it up to all of the running around I was doing at this conference. Once this lady got up from the table and left, however, my energy immediately returned. I realized, after meditating on this situation later, that the reason my energy drained around this lady was because she was projecting the negative energy she was currently feeling toward her daughter on to me since I reminded her so much of her daughter—thereby draining my positive energy. These people are sometimes called "energy vampires." I always thought that was a silly term for it but it is actually fairly accurate. This woman in particular was not doing this consciously, but her lower vibration thoughts and feelings about her daughter influenced my energy to the point of pulling it down from its higher vibration.

I have a relative who has a similar effect on me. When I am around this person for an extended period of time, I become very irritated and annoyed. Once I get to this state, I become short-tempered and am no longer enjoying myself around this person. And over time, I have learned my tolerance level with this person: I know my feelings of irritation begin around day three. Knowing this, I plan my visit accordingly, spending only two days with this individual so as to make the visit as pleasant for both of us as possible.

The book *Power vs. Force* by Dr. David Hawkin describes how everything has a vibration level, from people, to inanimate objects, to pictures. The higher vibration the person the more influence the vibration level has on that person and the people around it. Higher vibration energies can actually "cancel out" negative vibration energies—if they are high enough—thereby healing the person or situation with just their presence. The Masters Jesus and Buddha were two of these individuals. Their presence not only healed many individuals during their lifetime and even after, but animated and enlightened the individuals they came into contact with to new levels of being.

The higher you vibrate, the more you feel good and the closer you are to God. It is so much easier to maintain a sense of faith and trust life to take care of you when you are vibrating at a higher level. When you finally understand this and are aware of when your vibration is rising or falling, it becomes almost painful when you find yourself living in the lower vibrations, whether it is in certain places or with certain people. Feeling good becomes your top priority and the more you allow yourself to feel good, the higher you vibrate. When you do have moments where you feel down, you almost cannot stand to be there anymore so you do something immediately to feel better and raise your vibration back up. The more you make choices that are aligned with your spiritual contract, the higher you vibrate and the more you are living your life free of fear—because fear just doesn't exist in the higher vibrations.

USING YOUR EMOTIONS AS A GUIDE

"Nothing is more important than how you feel."
~Esther Hicks

Society has done a great job in teaching us that expressing our emotions is a sign of weakness and that feelings cannot be used to make sound-proof decisions. Women, and more so men, tend to often be criticized for showing their emotions in public.

Emotions are powerful tools…the most powerful tools we have for manifesting what we want in our lives. They are the language of the universe. If the emotions can be used as a guide rather than as a dirty secret, powerful transformations can happen not just in your own personal life but throughout our world. Our ability to feel deeply is what makes us human. If you feel something that you interpret as very bad, all that means is that at one point in your life you must have felt something very good or you would not know that this thing was "bad." All emotions have a place and a purpose. We need to feel the entire gamut of them in order to really experience being human. We tend to think that we should never feel bad, that bad feelings have no purpose. Remember, pain is one of our biggest motivators. As long as we are aware of what feeling we are experiencing, we should allow it to manifest instead of hiding it; then, we can use our feelings as tools to help us make decisions and to know where we are on our spiritual path.

Each emotion has a vibration. The emotions that feel the best— love, empowerment, joy—vibrate at a high level. Those emotions that we consider bad—anger, frustration, hate, depression—have a low vibration. Esther Hicks' "Emotional Guidance System." from her book *Ask And It Is Given* is the best tool I have seen yet for monitoring your vibration level using your feelings as a guide. The feelings are listed in order of the highest vibrating feelings of joy, love, and empowerment down to the lowest vibrating feelings of fear, grief, and depression. How do you use this powerful emotional vibration tool? Let's say you are going about your day and you are suddenly aware that you are feeling worried about losing your job. This is a worry for you because you lost your last job 6 months ago due to downsizing. Worry falls at number 14 on the emotional guidance system. Your vibration is now lower due to the fact that you are worrying. The goal is to raise your vibration any time you become aware that it is lower than where you want it to be.

HOW DO I RAISE MY VIBRATION?

Raising your vibration is easier than you may think. Take a moment and think about the times where you felt good. What were you doing? What were you thinking about? Make a list of things that you enjoy doing that make you feel better when you are down. These things can be anything: reading a book, talking to a specific friend, watching a movie, petting your cat, etc. The good news is your vibration level is totally in your control. You can raise or lower your vibration based on what you are feeling in the moment—and what you are feeling in the moment depends on what you are thinking and experiencing. This is why monitoring your thoughts is so important. If you want to feel good you have to think good thoughts that precipitate good feelings, hang around people that make you feel good, do things that make you feel good, and above all, think things that make you feel good.

Once you become aware you are feeling "bad," go to your supply of things you know you can do to make you feel better and do one of them immediately. I know what you are thinking…what if I am at work? I can't just stop working and do something else. Yes, you can! You can take a few deep diaphragmatic breaths (more on these later), you can go outside for a minute, you can walk around the office and move your body, you can talk to a co-worker who is positive, and so forth. Please don't limit yourself based on your environment. If necessary, make a separate list of things you can do to feel better at work if that helps.

Now that you have done one of these activities to help you feel better, check in to see what feeling you are experiencing now. Let's say you were feeling angry and now are feeling just frustrated. Still not a "good" feeling, but guess what: You have moved *up* the scale because frustration vibrates at a higher level than anger and that is the point. You want to move up the scale so you are moving up in vibration. Continue to be aware of your feelings. Remember, your main goal is to feel good!

YOUR EMOTIONAL VESSEL

Our emotions come from many places. They are triggered when memories surface from an experience we had in our past, they pop up when we experience something new, and many times they are created by our own thoughts, wandering in and out of the past and future. Have you ever met anyone before who seems emotionally numb? No matter what happens in their lives, you never see them express any kind of emotion, good or bad.

I dated a man once who was in an long-term relationship before he met me. Although we dated for only a short period of time, our relationship never had any emotional substance whatsoever. Steve had been in a relationship with his ex for 11 years, lived with her, helped raise her daughter, and had everything a married couple had although they never actually married. One day, Steve found out his girlfriend was seeing another man. He followed her to meet this man one night. Upon finding them together, out of shear rage, he proceeded to beat this man to a pulp—being an ex-Marine and a police officer, he was a very strong man. He proceeded to tell his girlfriend that she had 20 minutes to get back to the house and pack her things up or he would burn everything. She went back to the house, packed up her stuff, and he never saw or spoke to her or her daughter again. Steve had such a hard time getting over what happened and was so hurt that he checked himself into a hotel by the beach for a month where he proceeded to bury every emotion he ever had for this woman; he built a wall of solid brick that no one else would ever penetrate.

At the time I met Steve, it had been five years since this had happened. He was a very attractive man physically but was obviously angry at life. He could not show me any emotion whatsoever because he was afraid to feel anything for anyone after his experience with his ex. He spoke of the experience as if it had just happened yesterday.

All of our emotions sit in a vessel, if you will. They are contained here so we can call on them and use them whenever we need. This vessel is flexible and ever-changing depending on the store of emotions within it—emotions built from experiences we have had in our lifetime. In order to allow new emotions in, we have to release the old. If we hold on to old emotions and never release them, they fill up our vessel. When our vessel is full, no new emotions from our new experiences can enter. In Steve's case, he never fully healed and released the emotions from his last relationship, therefore he was unable (and too afraid) to allow new emotions to enter. There was no room in his vessel. Many individuals get stuck in this pattern. They hold onto anger, resentment, and bitterness so tightly that when a new experience comes along with good emotions, there is no place for the new emotions to go.

One of the most powerful lessons we can learn is to not let outside circumstances dictate our inner emotions. Our emotions are totally in our control, as long as we are aware of them. Never allow someone else to have that much power over you; don't let them enter that sacred space of your emotions and mess with them. When this happens, they are taking your power, and your vibration will lower. Your emotions are yours; never apologize for them because you have a right to them. Never make your decisions based on what other people think but on how it makes you feel. You cannot let the external—not just what people do or don't do, but also places, events, the weather, whatever—affect your emotions. Come from an empowered place; realize that the only reason your emotions are affecting you the way they are is because *you* are adding meaning to the experience based on some thought you are having that may not be the truth. Take back the reins of your life; decide how you want to feel and have the discipline to get yourself back on track. The divine knowledge you need to fulfill your contract can only flow when the emotional channels are open and not blocked by past emotions and conditioning.

NON-JUDGMENT

We have spent a lot of time talking about awareness and choice up to this point. Many of us, as we maneuver through the terrain of our lives, notice that our beliefs and choices vary from others, sometimes in a profound way. Others may make choices with which we do not agree—risky choices that may honor (or dishonor) them, depending on the choice.

We have all chosen in this lifetime to script others as our teachers, as well as having chosen to play a teacher ourselves. Through their behaviors and actions, others show us those things we need to pay attention to in our lives. When we witness the behaviors of others, we immediately compare what they are doing to what we ourselves would do or to what we have seen others do in the past. If these two do not match up, we tend to fall into judgment. We may criticize, condemn, and even ridicule others for the lack of knowledge and poor choice. How are we to know if that person isn't suppose to make that choice in order to learn a profound lesson? Who are we to judge?

When we are judging others, we are only judging ourselves. It is usually a behavior that we ourselves need to work on that annoys us when we see it in others. It is our own self-loathing, if you will, and for some reason we think if we condemn another we are off the hook.

It is what you do *after* you are aware of someone's behavior that judgment comes in. Judgment and observation are two very different things. If I am at a restaurant and I have poor service from the waiter, I can state the fact that poor service has been rendered and that is simply an observation. If I make the poor service personal to the waiter, saying it is probably because he has a tattoo on his arm and is from the lower end of town, that is a judgment.

I was visiting friends out of state recently and decided to pay a quick visit to some family I had in the area while I was there. On our way to meet my family, I stopped at a store to buy a few gifts with one of my friends. As I was standing in line, my friend and I began to have light conversation with an elderly African-American gentleman standing in line in front of me. When it was this gentleman's turn to check out, he carefully emptied his cart, the cashier rung him up, and when he went to reach for his wallet, he realized he had left it at home. Searching frantically in his pockets for any cash he had, he got tears of embarrassment in his eyes. Without thinking, I stepped up and swiped my credit card through the machine, turned to the gentleman and said, "It's your lucky day!" and proceeded to pay for his groceries. He protested several times and I turned to him, looked him in the eye, and simply said, "Just continue to pay it forward."

As this was going on, my friend, who was standing behind me watching me swipe my credit card, began to whisper my name very harshly and loudly. I ignored her until my conversation was done with the man; when I turned to her, she said, "You just paid for a black man's groceries! What are you doing!?" Being embarrassed and appalled by my friend's reaction, I told her we would talk in the car, paid for my own items, and we left the store. My friend proceeded to banter on about why I would possibly do that because he would have probably never done that for me, and how did I know that the man didn't do that on purpose so I would just pay for his groceries. I explained to my friend that the color of the man's skin did not matter to me; I saw a fellow human being in need and I would hope that my action, being witnessed by others around, would inspire them to do a good deed the next time they saw someone in need. No matter how hard I tried to explain, my friend could not get past the color of the man's skin to see the deeper meaning of the deed. She chose to put on her judgment hat and judged the man I helped based on her opinion and biases about people of color.

We also tend to put the judgment hat on when it comes to ourselves, being the judge and jury and getting out the noose to hang ourselves for every little mistake we make. Learn to practice the art of observation. Watch yourself and the choices you make from an observer point of view. Look at your life symbolically, always asking "What is really going on here?" "Why am I reacting this way to what he just said?" "Why am I all of a sudden feeling this way?" and "Why is this happening... again!?" This way of thinking puts you in a mode of watching your patterns. You begin to see where you are your own judge, where you are most hard on yourself, and where you need the most work. Journaling comes in extremely handy here when you are trying to identify patterns of thought and behaviors that need to be balanced or eliminated all together. Once you see a pattern, then you have a limiting belief (a lie) that you can then begin to re-frame.

Don't be afraid to call on your higher self to help here. Ask your higher self to "burn up" any thoughts that are not aligned with your highest purpose and get rid of them all together. Use your spiritual side to help with the re-programming. The Divine is always willing to step in when you need assistance. All you have to do is ask! There comes a time in everyone's life when you finally realize that we were never meant to do this thing called life alone…if we were, we wouldn't be surrounded by so many wonderful teachers in so many different disguises.

MANIFESTING

"Whatever it is you are feeling is a perfect reflection of what is in the process of becoming."
~Esther Hicks

There has been so much written on this topic recently that I think many have become confused as to what to do to truly create or make happen—to "manifest"—what they want in their lives. We have actually already indirectly discussed how to manifest, but let me make it simple for you.

Anything you want is made of matter. Matter is energy. Thought directs energy. Energy is pushed out to the Universe via our feelings. What you feel is what you manifest. Every time!

When you allow yourself to believe and really feel that what you want to manifest can and will come to you, then the Universe meets you half way and lines up events to allow what you want to become real. I recently decided to move to Scottsdale, Arizona from Rising Sun, Maryland…quite the big move considering I have a grandchild on the way, a daughter starting college, and a thriving business on the east coast. It has been a dream of mine to move out west for quite some time so I decided to make it happen. I believed with all of my heart that the details would fall into place and I would be guided to the things and people I needed to make this move happen. Ironically, I recently was having a conversation with a friend of mine who lives in Arizona with whom I have worked in the past and she mentioned that she also wanted to move to Scottsdale. We decided to move in together and we proceeded to look for a place to live. My friend found a house for rent in the perfect location that she just happened to see a year ago. We applied for the house and waited patiently, hoping our application would get approved. The next day, I received an email from my personal assistant who lives in Pennsylvania that was titled, "You won't believe this!" She proceeded to tell me that the man who owns the house my friend and I were trying to rent in Arizona is her next door neighbor in Pennsylvania! He was looking over my application, went to my website to see what I do for a living and saw my assistant's name. He proceeded to call her, got a glowing unsolicited reference of me and offered us the house. A perfect example of how the Universe meets you half way.

The reason you do not manifest what it is you want in your life is due to the fact that your attention is focused on everything *but* what you want to manifest. You spend more time feeling fearful around the thought of "what if it doesn't happen" than focusing on the feelings of how it will feel when it actually manifests into your life.

"What you think and what you feel and what manifests is always a match."
-Esther Hicks

Manifestation is mainly a function of focus. Where we put our focus determines what we will receive. In our current third dimension reality, vibrations move more slowly than they do in higher planes. The higher planes of existence are where your higher self resides—the higher self we are tapping into to manifest. We are blessed with a buffer of time in third dimension. This serves us well because often what we think and feel is *not* what we want to manifest; we are not actually thinking and feeling what we want to see in our lives. The key to manifesting is holding your focus long enough to manifest that which you want.

The majority of the time people do not hold their focus long enough to manifest anything except their fears and worries. Using your faith while you hold your focus and remaining, as you wait, in a state of expectation and gratitude brings forward your manifestation. If you hold an image of the life you want, that image will eventually become fact.

You may wonder if this means that all of the unhappy and negative things you see in your life are your fault because you're focusing on the wrong things? If you see the worst around you, it is because that is where you are focusing. And here is the lesson learned: You must now take accountability and responsibility for your life situation up to this point. It is what you created. It may not be what you wanted, but it is what you created nonetheless. There is no need to grieve it, be angry about it, or feel guilty. It is what it is; now change it! Take the lesson and leave the experience behind. The strong don't wait for opportunities, they create them. Stop waiting for someone or something to give you permission to go get what you want. It is never because of someone or something that you don't have what you want. No one can control you that much. You are always, always, always in control of your own buttons. No one else chooses how you want to feel, what you want to create, what you want to do, where you want to go. That's up to you.. If the illusion is that they are controlling you, then that is simply because you are allowing them. You are giving them your power. STOP!! The circumstances will never be more perfect than they are right now to go after your dreams. Any other excuse for not moving toward your dreams is simply that: an excuse.

"You do not need to leave your room. Remain sitting quietly at your table and listen. Do not even listen, simply wait. Do not even wait, be quiet, still and solitary. The world will freely offer itself to you to be unmasked; it has no choice. It will roll in ecstasy at your feet."
-Franz Kafka

CHAPTER TEN

YOU ARE NOT ALONE

"God doesn't give you the people you want; he gives you the people you NEED...to help you, to hurt you, to leave you, to love you, and to make you into the person you were meant to be."

OUR "TEACHERS"

God has placed a lot of farmers in our lives who plant seeds to help us along our path. These individuals are there for a specific reason. They are there to help us by teaching us lessons we cannot teach ourselves. They offer us experiences that teach us what we need to learn to take the next step forward on our journey.

Let's imagine for a moment that you have not yet been born. When you sit with your guides and angels to script the lessons you want to learn for this lifetime, there are several others involved in the process. Over the many lifetimes you have lived, you have individuals that are your soul mates. The term "soul mate" has been grossly misused over the centuries. A soul mate is someone with whom we have shared many, many lifetimes. He or she is someone who is in our "soul group." A soul group is a cluster of souls who have traveled together throughout time. Soul mates are individuals who are part of our soul group and play the main "characters," if you will, in the script we have created—much like the actors who have come together to create a movie.

There are several ways to know when we have come across these individuals. One way is when we have the experience of meeting someone for the first time and feeling as if we already know them. We usually have one of two feelings: We either immediately like them or immediately dislike them, and we don't know why. The other way we know them is by looking at the type of relationship we have with that person. Is that person teaching you a valuable lesson either through pain or through a valued relationship? If the answer is yes, then that person is one of your soul mates. These individuals come in and out of our lives. When their "role" is finished, they will leave one way or another. Sometimes we want them to leave and just "know" it is time, such as a friend with whom you just don't seem to have much in common anymore; at other times, they leave when we don't want them too, such as a significant other in a romantic relationship breaking up with you or someone passing away.

"When people walk away from you, let them go. Your destiny is never tied to anyone who leaves you, and it doesn't mean they are bad people. It just means that their part in your story is over."
~Tony Mc Collum

SOUL IMPERATIVES

We all have "soul imperatives," or unfinished business that we have the opportunity to resolve in every lifetime we live. These soul imperatives operate unconsciously to motivate our present life and include past life promises and purposes that drive our soul forward from life to life. This imperative draws partners back into our orbit in the guise of lovers or enemies, all of which serve a purpose to move our soul forward on our journey toward ascension.

*"When you say good-bye to someone or decide not to see them
again, remember you are a moment in their story. Make it a story
that doesn't leave a scar."*
~Charlotte Kasl, "If the Buddha Dated"

My friend Elaine came into my life at a very unique time. My father had just passed away the year before and we met through a mutual friend. Elaine was taking a class with this friend and asked him if he knew anyone who could give her a more spiritual base to what she was learning. He referred her my way and we met briefly at an expo. We decided to get together for coffee the following week and three hours later, we were still talking. Elaine and I became fast friends. We spoke every day on the phone, sometimes more than once a day and quickly learned everything about each other. We later realized that we had specific roles that we were supposed to play for each other. I was just beginning the process of getting a divorce and she had been there and done that. She was my rock and confidant the entire year I was divorcing. Once my divorce was over, her father, who had been ill, passed away. This time, *I* had been there and done that. Now it was my turn to be her rock and voice of experience.

We remained friends, and still remain best friends to this day, but our friendship has shifted continuously throughout the years. We slowly drifted apart at times, not spending as much time together as before. Our roles, being complete for the time being, forced us to "move on" to allow other soul mates to enter to teach us our next lessons. Then there would be times when we would be much more present in each other's lives.

When you can learn that all of the relationships that drift in and out of your life exist for a reason—a specific purpose to show you something, teach you something, or force you to move along your path—your perspective on these individuals will shift dramatically. Your "enemies" and those that cause you the most pain become your greatest teachers. Forgiveness becomes easier and you begin to watch the flow of your life take you toward and away from the exact people and situations you need at that time.

"Every single person who drifted in and out of your life is a part of your divinely chosen experience. As you move into the world of inspiration, you will find it easy...and even necessary...to give thanks for all of these people, and to take serious note of what they brought you."
~Wayne Dyer

YOU ARE NEVER ALONE

Some people come into our lives and quickly go.
Some people move our souls to dance.
They awaken us to new understanding with the
passing whisper of their wisdom.
Some people make the sky more beautiful to gaze upon.
They stay in our lives for awhile, leave footprints on our
hearts and we are never, ever the same.

When we are going through transformational times in our lives, it is not uncommon that we may feel a degree of loneliness. Self-despair kicks in and we feel as if we are the only ones on the planet, that no one really cares about us, and we may even go as far as secluding ourselves from the rest of the world for a bit. Solitude time is extremely important as you raise your vibration level. It is in solitude that you have time to sit in silence, become aware of and hear the thoughts in your mind that haunt you so secretly throughout the day, and then re-frame those thoughts to thoughts that don't haunt you but raise you up.

It is important in these times to remember that you are never really alone. Just because you cannot see anyone does not mean that no one is there. We all have guides and angels with us constantly, some assigned solely to us to help us on our journey and others on "temporary assignment" to help us get through a certain phase of our journey.

Our guides are there to help us complete our destiny and fulfill the promises we made to God—to fulfill our contract, so to speak. They only provide guidance and it is up to us whether we choose to listen or not and how we choose to use that guidance. Moses, my Master guide, tells me to think of them as a library…a plethora of information but only providing you the guidance you need at the time. One thing we need to remember is that we are on a need-to-know basis here on Earth. We are given information to help us make our choices, but because we have free will, too much information may affect the choice we make. Guides are not allowed to "interfere" with our choices. They are here as teachers who have been in our shoes before and guide us gently along our highest path.

Our guides are just one of the many tools our Creator has given us to help us make our highest choices in this lifetime. All that is needed is a sense of belief: belief that we are not alone on this journey and that a much higher source than us believes in us and our choices beyond anything we can possibly imagine.

Many feel that being able to hear guidance from guides and angels is a gift only a few are given. This is not true. We all have intuition. We all have guides and angels and they speak to us in their own unique language and in a way *we* will understand. We receive guidance and messages in many ways: dreams; a complete stranger we happen to sit next to on a plane; a billboard; an instantaneous thought that comes out of nowhere; a vision we receive right before we wake up in the morning; and so many more. We just have to be open to the possibility that we are not alone and are surrounded by a world full of angels that want to help us make our best choices.

If you want to practice getting to know your guides and angels, take some time every day, preferably in the morning, and just simply sit with your eyes closed. Visually surround your body with white light and ask your Master guide to come to your left or right side. Be fully present and notice in that moment what you feel. Do you feel a temperature change? A tingly sensation in your arm? A flutter in your heart? Did an image pass through your mind quickly? Did you hear anything in your head? Did you smell anything? Do this every morning for several days and you will eventually begin to learn the "language" that you and your guides share. You will know when they are around and you will also begin to trust the feelings you get in response to pleas for guidance.

We are given signs all of the time that remind us that we are not alone. I hike the area around Mount Shasta in California quite a bit; after one hike, I laid my coat on the snow-covered ground, stuck my walking poles in the snow next to me, and sat down to eat my lunch. As I sat there looking up at the mountain, a bird landed right on top of one of my poles, starred at me for a few seconds as if she had something to say, and then flew off. Now just to give you a frame of reference for how odd this was, the area at the base of Mount Shasta is surrounded by pine trees… hundreds and hundreds of pine trees! It is not like the bird didn't have any place else to land! I chose to believe this was a cute little sign telling me I was not alone on that mountain and was being "watched."

In your heart, know you are never alone. Those that surround us are the ones that offer to us the gifts and lessons we need to move forward towards our ascension. We just have to be open to receive them.

RECEIVING

As you raise your vibration and begin to develop your psychic gifts, allowing yourself to be open to receiving is of utmost importance. The reason why self-esteem and self-worth are so critical during this process is due to the fact that when you feel good about yourself and feel worthy, you are receptive. Liking yourself is akin to opening doors to the Universe. You open doors to allow yourself to receive guidance, to receive help, and to receive miracles. These gifts only make themselves known if you are in a state of pure reception: no judgment, no expectation, simply open to receiving whatever the Divine has to offer. When we trust the Universe and trust our sacred contract, we trust that whatever comes our way is meant to come our way "as is." Receiving these nuggets from the Divine openly and unabashedly allows more guidance and gifts to enter. The Universe senses the open vibration, and because it works according to the law of attraction, it sends you more to receive.

Also, remember that receiving is not selfish. The Universe is always trying to balance itself so if you always give and never receive, there is no balance. Just as you need to exhale as much as you need to inhale, you need to receive as much as you need to give. When you allow yourself to receive, you give others a chance to balance their Universe by giving. If you find yourself feeling guilty about receiving, remember how Jesus lived while he walked the Earth. He openly received food, water, shelter, and love from so many that crossed on his path. He allowed them to show their love for him by giving. Imagine how they would have felt if Jesus had a problem with receiving and told them, "No thanks, I'm good!" We were all put here together to support and love each other... no one is meant to walk their path alone.

CHAPTER ELEVEN

ACTION STEPS TO JOY

"There's a Hole in My Sidewalk"

Chapter One

"I walk down a street and there's a big hole. I don't see it and fall into it. It's dark and hopeless and it takes me a long time to find my way out. It's not my fault!"

Chapter Two

"I walk down the same street. There's a big hole and I can see it, but I still fall in. It's dark and hopeless and it takes me a long time to get out. It's still not my fault."

Chapter Three

"I walk down a street. There's a big hole. I can see it, but I still fall in. It's become a habit. But I keep my eyes open and get out immediately. It is my fault."

Chapter Four

"I walk down a street. There's a big hole. And I walk around it."

Chapter Five

"I walk down a different street."

~Unknown

KNOWING YOURSELF

In order to be able to clearly know what you want and make the highest choices, you have to know yourself. This is the place where most of us get lost. Many people lose themselves in their lives, in their kids, in their significant other, and so forth, to the point that when they do have free time, they do the laundry!

Take the time to ask yourself: Do you know yourself and if you feel as if you don't, how do you get to know yourself again?

Start by making a list of all of the things you like to do. If nothing comes to mind, which often happens when your life has been lost for so long by giving to others and not to yourself, think of what you liked to do in the past. Make two lists: the first one with things you like to do at home that make you feel good or better when you are down, and the second one with things you can do at work to make yourself feel better. Whenever you find you have a spare moment (stop laughing!) or you become aware that you are feeling "bad" for some reason, take out this list and pick something from it to do *immediately*! The items on your list don't have to be time-consuming. They can include actions as quick and simple as taking five deep diaphragmatic breathes, listening to a song, calling a friend, taking a walk outside, or getting a cup of tea or coffee. Do anything that makes you feel better and get in touch with yourself. The more you do this, the more you will want to feel good. And that is the point: The more you feel good, the more you know you are in touch with yourself. Everyone's list is completely different. What I like to do or what makes me feel good is very different from what you like to do or what makes you feel good. Just go with it!

Now that you have your list, make sure that *every day* you take some time for yourself (and not just when you are in the bathroom!). And that doesn't mean just taking time for yourself "when you have the time." Admit it, that is what you are doing now and you *never* "have the time!" If something is important enough to you, you will make the time. Remember, you only take care of what you value. Value yourself enough to take the time to take care of YOU!

By slowing bringing awareness back to yourself, you will get to know who you are again. That person may be very different from the person you knew 10 or 20 years ago. That's ok. What's important is that you are moving forward. If you find that you have moved backward, that is ok, too. All you have is this moment and the choices you make that will shape your future. Leave the past where it belongs: in the past. Take the lesson you learned to make better choices in the future and leave the experience behind. Remember that fear only exists in the past and the future; it does not exist in the now. Use the now to your benefit and start to build the "you" that you have always wanted to become.

RELEASE

Whenever you are faced with a situation in your life that you do not like you have three choices: change it, leave it or accept it. Sometimes just making a choice relieves some of the pain. Either way, you need to learn the divine art of "release."

Our emotions are contained in a "vessel" within us. When the vessel gets too full, due to old feelings we are holding onto that we just won't let go of, there is no room in our vessel for new, beautiful feelings to enter. We must learn to release those things in our lives that no longer serve a purpose for our highest good. Just as you need to release toxins from your physical body, you need to also release toxins from your emotional body as well.

Release can take many forms. It doesn't matter what form you choose, as long as the end result is that you feel better.

- Laugh
- Cry
- Help someone else get what they want or feel better
- Be grateful for what you DO have in your life – start a gratitude journal
- Pray and/or Meditate
- Ask for help
- Sleep
- Read positive material that relates to your situation
- Talk about it to a friend to get feedback, not to dwell on it
- Take a hot bath or shower or swim—visualize your worries being "washed away"
- Move your body! Do some sort of physical activity
- Breathe (take several deep breaths pushing your bellybutton out instead of raising your chest – this is diaphragmatic breathing)
- Be in nature – nature is an automatic balancer
- Spend time with an animal – animals only know unconditional love

This list can go on and on. The important thing is to know what it is to do that makes you feel better. We all have our favorite things. The better you feel, the higher you are vibrating; the higher you are vibrating, the closer you are to God. We are never alone. Even in our most desperate moments, when there seems to be no one physically around, you can feel the arms of a deceased loved one or an angel wrapped around you like a warm blanket, filling your heart with hope, love, and the knowing that all will be ok.

ABOUT ANGER

I feel the need here to bring up a touchy subject and one that is not only part of the grieving process but a form of release as well. Anger is a natural emotional mechanism for dealing with loss and pain. Many believe expressing anger is bad to the extent that some people cannot even access the emotion (most of us perfectionists have an issue expressing anger), and for others it is expressed in a violent unhealthy way due to past conditioning. When anger is expressed in a healthy, normal way it is one of the best emotional release mechanisms there is.

Unfortunately, you see many people in our society stuck in anger and the "victim role." The victim role is one that is the easiest to play because it is the only role where you do not have to take responsibility or be held accountable for what you chose to create in your life by your words, actions, and choices (or lack of choices). You feel you have a right to be angry.

Anger is one of those emotions that can be good or bad. Good anger mobilizes you into action. When the doctors told me I could not control my illness, it angered me to the point where my entire focus was, "I'll show them!" That was mobilizing anger that helped me heal. Releasing pent-up anger to something that was done to you as a child and is affecting your behavior today as an adult is another healthy show of anger. This release can take the form of writing a letter to the person who wronged you and burning it as a symbol of releasing it "once and for all," going to the gym and punching the crap out of a punching bag, screaming in your pillow, crying and telling your story to a trusted friend, or pulling a "Forest Gump" and running until you can't run any more.

The other kind of anger is the anger that immobilizes you and causes you to freeze in your tracks—physically, emotionally and mentally. You constantly repeat in your mind the scenario that caused you so much anger: You blame; you judge; you make the other person wrong; and worst of all, you give your power away to a person or situation in the past that has you still gripped in the present. You are blind to solutions and deaf to prayer. You are so energetically "heavy" that even when solutions do appear, you don't see them and your vibration is closed down to receiving any gifts that may present themselves in the form of miracles. I believe it was Buddha who once said that anger (in this form) is like holding a hot coal in your hand: The only person who gets burned is you.

WHAT DON'T YOU WANT

One other way to get more in touch with yourself and what you want is to start by making a list of what you don't want. This is sometimes an easier place to start. Think of every area in your life and make a list of what you don't want—from relationships, to career, to money…to everything!

The easy next step is to then reverse the things you do not want and translate them into what you do want. This is an important step: Remember that what you think about expands, so you want to put more focus on what you want than what you don't want.

BUCKET LIST

"The only answers for YOU are in YOU. Jesus said, 'If you want to find life, you've got to look inside of YOU.'"
-Leo Buscaglia

Everyone should create a "Bucket List" or "Dream Inventory." A bucket list is a list of all of the things you want to do in your life before you "kick the bucket." As for the rules to creating a bucket list, it's simple: There are no rules! I tell my clients to pretend that their Fairy Godmother is sitting at the top of their paper waiting to grant anything that they write on their list. This helps you keep an open mind. Write down anything at all that comes to mind, no matter what! Don't worry about "how" it will manifest, if it is "realistic" (what does that really mean anyway), or what other people will think. Just write it down.

Be aware of any thoughts that pop up that make you hesitate writing something down on your bucket list. Make a note of these thoughts because they are the thoughts that are more than likely keeping you from your dreams. They are your limiting beliefs or your mental obstacles.

As your list becomes longer and longer, it will become easier and easier to find things to put on your list. Keep your eyes and ears open throughout each day to find things that resonate with what you want. Listen to the radio, flip through magazines, surf the Internet, listen to other people's conversations, and so on. See what animates you.

Many people at this point have a hard time because they feel they are being materialistic. Anything can go on your bucket list, not just material things. You can have items that relate to the types of characteristics you want to possess, further education, travel, restaurants at which you would like to eat, or instruments you would like to learn to play, just to name a few.

My friend Donna and I are bucket list buddies. We both have separate bucket lists but find the things on our lists that are the same and make spontaneous plans to experience them together. For example, we experienced New Year's Eve in Times Square to ring in 2011 and then 3 months later helped ring in Fat Tuesday at Mardi Gras in New Orleans! Both experiences were fabulous!

As you write your bucket list, make sure the things on there are as specific as you can make them. Your subconscious mind responds best to specifics. Next, put a star next to those things you think you can accomplish within the next 6 months to a year.

At the end of every year before the next one begins, I look at my bucket list and choose the things on it I would like to accomplish in the coming year. I write them all down on a separate list and make a vision board that hangs in my office with pictures of all of the things I plan on doing that coming year.

VISION BOARDS

Why do vision boards work? Because your subconscious mind thinks in pictures. If I say to you "chocolate cake," what comes to your mind? The *word* "chocolate cake" or a *picture* of an amazingly delicious cake? The picture, correct? The picture needs to be exactly what you want. Same color, size, shape, everything. Don't be fooled by your subconscious mind. It takes *exactly* what it sees and brings it to pass.

In November of 2009, I had the privilege of spending a couple of weeks in South Africa for a speaking engagement. The week before I left, my youngest daughter was standing in my office waiting for me to get off of the phone (as usual!) and was looking at my vision board. When I got off of the phone, she said to me, "Mom, did you realize South Africa is on your vision board?" I turned around and looked and there was a picture of elephants from a safari and the words "South Africa" above it. I had actually forgotten it was there. Then she said, "What is so cool Mom is that you didn't even try to make that happen, it just happened on its own!" Brilliant girl! And that is exactly how it happens. When you take the time to define what you want and then have a visual of it, you make it easy on your subconscious mind to act on what you want. It taps into your higher self and the powers that be and makes it happen in conjunction with the Universe, whether you like it or not! That is the power of your subconscious mind.

It is important to know what you want but it is not necessary to obsess about your wants in order for them to manifest in your life. Sometimes, focusing too much on the form you want a manifestation to take actually inhibits the Universe and its ability to aid you in creating it in your life. You must learn to release the hold you have on the form you want it to take and how you think is the best way for it to manifest. These two things are not up to you. They are up to the Universe. When we release the form of what we wish to create, the Universe provides the perfect form for its manifestation, and you in turn get exactly what you want...and faster!

10-YEAR PROJECTION

Another excellent way to help define what you want is to do a 10-year projection exercise. This can be a bit tricky but is very worth the effort. Shoot yourself out 10 years into the future and define exactly what you want to see in your life. Where do you want to be working? What do you want to be doing? Who do you want to be with? How much money do you want to be making? Make sure when you do this exercise you are describing your life how you *want* it to be, not how you think it *will* or *should* be. If 10 years is too long, than project out 5 years.

The exercise below is the one I use with my clients to help them define the future they want. If you are not able to complete this exercise initially, simply keep coming back to it until you can reach the end.

The first part of the exercise is to imagine the future. Fill in the following information:

1. In ten years my age is…

2. My occupation is (be as specific as possible)…

3. My approximate annual income is…

4. The three biggest changes I have made in my life over the past 10 years are…

5. My three greatest accomplishments over the past 10 years are…

6. Of my experiences in the last few years, the ones that gave me the greatest sense of accomplishment were…

7. In reviewing my "Ten-Year Projection," the most important observations I made were…

Once you have imagined the future, return to the present. The purpose of this part of the exercise is to aid you in drawing together information about yourself. You can use this information when you set goals.

Ask yourself the following, considering what you are doing now:

8. If you were to continue to live your life the way you are living it right now, what would it cost you?

9. What is giving you the greatest sense of accomplishment?

10. What is giving you the least sense of accomplishment?

11. What are your greatest strengths?

12. What areas in your life need improvement?

13. Many people have a "secret dream" in their life. What is your "secret dream?"

14. Many of us would like to have the freedom to do the things we want to do when we want to do them. What would you do if you had:

One Hour?

One Day?

One Week?

One Year?

15. What would you like your tombstone to say about you?

16. Looking back on this exercise, what is the thing that motivates you the most to take action?

Once you have completed the above exercises, think about what your ideal day would be in the future. Pretend that it is now 10 years in the future. You have just awakened and are excited because you are going to have your favorite kind of day today.

1. What kind of clothing are you putting on?
2. What does your house look like?
3. Where are you going today?
4. What are you eating for breakfast?
5. Who will you be spending time with?
6. What job do you have?

Write out as much as you can in detail and be as specific as you can about what your life will look like 10 years from now. Use the same idea as when you did your bucket list. Take off the blinders and don't worry about how it will happen…just write it as if it is already a given in 10 years.

(parts of exercise courtesy of Resource Associates Corporation)

KNOWING WHERE YOU ARE

Many find it fun to do a bucket list and think about all of the things they want in their lives. But many also find it frustrating. We have all set goals and thought about things we have wanted in our lives. Many of those things have come to pass but many of them have not. If you're wondering why, ask yourself this question: *What is guiding what you do and don't do in your life: your dreams or your fears?* Many people live their lives based on their fears and not their dreams. They constantly make excuses for why they cannot do what they want. From my own clients, I hear everything from "I have responsibilities" or "that just isn't realistic to think that way" to "I would rather do things for other people than myself."

One of the main reasons we do not accomplish the goals we set is because we never truly define *from where we are starting.* It is great to have the end in mind, but you have to know where your beginning is as well. If I got in my car and wanted to drive to Los Angeles and did not know from where I was leaving, I would not know which way to go – east, west, north or south. I would not know how long it would take to get there. You must take the time to define from where you are starting. How do you feel about yourself in every area of your life? At what level is your self-esteem? Do you like yourself? Do you value yourself?

Once you have your bucket list and know from where you are starting...then the fun begins!

PRIORITIES

"Every action and expenditure of energy should be in alignment with your priorities and your purpose."

If I asked you to identify the top three priorities in your life right now, would you be able to answer? Many cannot. Many do not take the time to think about this question.

Priorities are those things that are important to you *at this moment*. I stress "at this moment" because your priorities do and will change depending on what is going on in your life. When I became ill, my physical health became a top priority immediately! If you start a new job, that may be your top priority at the moment. Life happens but what is most important is to make sure that as life is "happening," your focus stays on those things that you feel are most important to you. You want your energies focused in the direction of your priorities and in that direction only! That is true balance. Balance is not a perfect 50/50 split of work and home; balance is knowing your priorities and putting your energy towards those priorities every day to some degree. We feel bad about ourselves when we know we have not spent time on what is important to us.

Your priorities are yours and yours only. There is no right or wrong answer to what you feel is important. Allow yourself to explore this part of you. Revisit your priorities often. Make sure they are in alignment with what you want and what makes you feel good. And most of all, make sure your daily energies are focused on those priorities. That is where you should be spending most of your time and energy.

The other benefit of knowing your priorities is that it makes decision-making so much easier. When my dad was dying of cancer, I immediately made him my top priority. I thought to myself: I don't want him to pass away and spend the rest of my life saying to myself, "I wish I would have…" At the time my dad was sick, my parents lived in Cleveland while I lived in Maryland. It didn't matter; whenever the phone rang with news that my dad was in the hospital again, it would take me two seconds to make my decision of where I should be because I knew my priorities. Yes, I had a family to take care of at home and was a traveling, in-demand speaker and facilitator, so I had to make arrangements. I spoke with my husband and girls about the possibility of mom leaving to see grandpa when I was needed to make sure they understood why I was doing what I was doing. It was very important to me that they understood that I was not there for them because I wanted to be with grandpa while he was in this critical stage of his illness.. That way there was no question as to why mom was not around. I also let my clients know I was dealing with an ongoing family emergency and if something came up and I couldn't speak, I would make sure someone would be there in my place. Covering all the bases gave me peace of mind and those in my life peace of mind as well.

You cannot wait for life to come to you…you have to go to it! In order to do that, you need to be able to define what you want. What type of person do you want to be? Where do you want to live? Where do you want to go? What do you want your relationships to be like? How do you want to feel? In order to find your life, you have to live it… making mistakes along the way…feeling the pain of sorrow, loss, joy, love, and ecstasy of it all.

"Your life lies underneath your life situation."
~ *Eckart Tolle*

The situation in which you currently find yourself is the vehicle that is showing you how to live. It is the teacher of the lesson. Your only job is to be present so you can see what it is life is trying to show you. You need to show up for your life if you want to live it.

OTHER PEOPLE'S REACTION TO THE "NEW YOU"

"How can I be me if I do not let you be you?
One person's "music" can change the world!"
~*Wynton Marsalis*

Once you begin to embark on your journey of self-discovery there will be many things about you that will change—some subtle, and some not so subtle. You will begin to feel different in your own skin and literally become addicted to "feeling good." You will vaguely remember how you "used to be," and looking back will give you a serene sense of accomplishment in seeing how far you have come.

Others, on the other hand, may not immediately join in on the celebration. Certain habits and behaviors that once ran as commonplace in your persona no longer exist. Some of these behaviors, even though they didn't benefit you, made other's lives easier…at your expense. When those behaviors change and become in balance with honoring yourself, you will get mixed reactions from those who no longer benefit from your new behaviors. As I put it when I finally started to honor myself and "draw some lines in the sand," I was finally "in the equation" of my life. How many times do you make a decision based on what is best for everyone else in your life, *except for you*? Do you ever consider what you want, what will make life easier for you or what is convenient for you when you make a decision? In the past, having little or no self-esteem, you may have answered these questions with a "No," but now, you are in the equation. You regard and love yourself enough to matter to the person whose opinion matters the most…YOU!

When I was newly divorced, I noticed that I had to "redefine" many of the relationships in my life—relationships with my family, my friends, and even my daughters. Certain friends were no longer comfortable spending time with me. Some felt awkward because they only knew me as "part of a couple." For some of my friends, I was a reminder of a life they wish they had the courage to pursue, but didn't; many of them in unhappy marriages themselves. I also realized, with my daughters in particular, that certain behavior patterns I ran were the same ones I ran with my ex-husband. For instance, I always felt as if everyone else's happiness was my responsibility. I created this circumstance by always sacrificing my desires and my time to make everyone else happy and comfortable. Once I decided that this pattern no longer served me in my marriage, I began to see how I ran that pattern with other individuals in my life, mainly with my daughters. I realized my "no" was never "no." They would ask me a question regarding some place they wanted to go or something they wanted to do and I would say no; then the "wearing down" process began. They would continue to ask why and give me every rationalization in the book for why it was a good idea that I say "yes" and I would eventually give in. This interaction always left me feeling frustrated and annoyed. I realized the frustration was never really directed at my girls but at myself for constantly caving and sacrificing myself to "make them happy." When my "no" finally became an actual "no" they, of course, did not have a pleasant reaction. Those closest to us know exactly what buttons to push in us to get us going, from the guilt button all the way to the tears button. As my girls tried frantically to push every button they could in me to no avail, they finally would end up angry, not necessarily at me but at the fact that the old pattern of our relationship no longer worked. I now was making them step up to the plate and change something about their behavior to meet me "half way" instead of me always going the whole distance. The road was bumpy for a while and I was not perfect in my new stance at first, but eventually they got used to the "new me," and most importantly, began to respect my new behavior. In honoring myself with this new behavior I also was indirectly holding up a higher "version of self" for my daughters as well. I was allowing them the opportunity to be a "bigger person" and find a new solution to dealing with a change that had occurred—a wonderful life lesson for them as well. Today, I think we respect each other more than ever before.

One of the benefits of having high self-esteem is that you simply cease caring what others think anymore. Their opinions just don't matter. The only opinion that holds any weight for you is your own. This is a critical piece of the transformational process because worrying about what others think has driven so many of our behaviors for our whole lives. Before I leave for any solo journey I take, I always have well-intentioned people say things to me such as: "Be careful..I worry about you traveling alone"; "Aren't you afraid to travel alone?"; and my all-time favorite, "It really isn't safe for a woman to travel alone." If I worried about what others thought of me, I would never have taken any of the many journeys that have been so transformational. I would have been robbed of those experiences simply because others felt they needed to rub their own fears off on me—and that is exactly what other people do. We can only ever perceive life from our own experiences, fears, and dreams. It is none of our business what other people think of us and what we do anyway.

"The best time, in fact the only time, to make a real change in your life is in the moment of seeing a need for it. He who hesitates always gets lost in the hundred reasons why tomorrow is a better day to get started."
~Guy Finley

EPILOGUE

I was guided one day, after reading *"The Wheel of Life,"* by Elizabeth Kübler-Ross, to share some things I learned from Elizabeth's book with my dad. I remember the moment well. I was sitting on the sofa as he sat in the chair in which he always sat in our family living room. He had been very quiet for several days, not speaking to anyone, not watching TV, just sitting and apparently staring into space. I asked him point blank if he wanted to talk about dying and if he had any fears and that I would be happy to talk to him about, or just listen. He looked over at me and said, "I am not afraid to die, Chris." But as he said the words, I saw fear in his eyes. I proceeded to tell him about the four phases of dying I had just read about in Elizabeth's book, taking a chance I would not scare him. My dad's beliefs were very much based on Catholicism and a slight lack of believing in a spirit world. I also had the distinct feeling he had done some things in his life he never shared with anyone of which he may not have been too proud. (I learned for the first time a few months before he died that my father had been in Vietnam). I went on to talk about what I believed and tried to reassure him there was nothing to fear.

Sometimes in life, and obviously in death as well, it is hard for us to hold in front of ourselves those things of which we are not proud, those choices we made that maybe did not serve the ultimate good or may have hurt others around us—or even those we did not know. The true test of any choice is whether or not you would make that choice again. The beauty of this is that we can hold these past choices in front of ourselves and truly look at them for what they are: an opportunity to learn a lesson. We can then go forward, taking the lesson and leaving the experience behind, so that we can make wiser choices of a higher vibration going forward the next time. My good friend and spiritual mentor, Pat, describes it as the same process we use when we go to clean out our closet. In order to know whether or not we want to keep or get rid of something, we need to take it out of the closet and look at it first; then we decide if it stays in the closet or gets discarded. Once this decision is made we can forgive ourselves and move on.

By learning from our past choices, we can eventually know we lived up to our highest potential and did the best we possibly could— we know that we made the highest possible choices at all times along our journey. And for those times we did not make such wise choices, we know we were able to learn from those choices and move forward with our heads held high, certain that we would make better choices in the future. This is the power and the beauty of human will. We can choose to stumble and mess up, but we can also choose to mend, forgive, learn, and love. As one of my guides so wisely stated, "Free choice is the highest gift man received when he was born into planet Earth. Every moment you make choices in your speaking, doing, and thinking, all of them are terribly important. Each choice affects every life form on the planet." Everyone finds their own path to God. I personally do not believe in a judgmental God or one that has rules and punishes you for "breaking the rules" or making the "wrong choice." The God I have experienced is one of Divine light, pureness and unconditional love. He wants our hearts to be filled with joy and love and to know, no matter what we choose, he loves us anyway. We are all put here as small extensions, pieces if you will, of our Divine creator, all for the purpose of coming back to our true Divine selves at the end of this journey…to finally remember who we are and why we came here. When we choose to do something with love in our hearts and a Divine intention, the choice is never wrong, regardless of what is written in our many spiritual texts. Everything comes back to intention and our feelings. That is what drives the love in our hearts to God's heart. When we choose to love each other, we are loving God. It is really just that simple.

A few months before my dad passed, I asked him for a favor. With all of the conversations he and I had shared regarding death and dying, fear and life, I asked if when he died, he could show me a sign to let me know whether or not anything we had discussed about death was true.

I had no doubt, but I wanted to show him I also questioned and it was okay. I wanted to give him something to look forward to. He agreed. What I got a few months later was more than an answer.

Ten months after my dad passed I finally felt ready to re-engage in my spiritual work. I called Pat and asked her if she could sit with me and my guides and help me interpret some messages I was receiving that were just not clear. Sometimes, when we are very emotionally attached to a situation, the guidance we are receiving is clouded by the emotions we are feeling, and it is sometimes not always clear. I have learned in these times that it is helpful to call upon the friends who have awakened these gifts to help me interpret my messages. Pat is one of those friends.

I sat in Pat's office and almost immediately my father appeared to her with an urgent message for me. What my father proceeded to say completely brought me to my knees. He said he remembered our conversation and that it was amazing to him that "consciousness does survive death." When we pass we are welcomed by our angels and guides who escort us to "the other side"; as we are traveling we are greeted by all of our loved ones who have passed and we finally feel as if we are "home." All of the pain, worry, and fear just dissolve into the unconditional love that is felt from all of the people present on this journey. We are given a life review and are able to see what impact the choices we made had on our lives and also the lives of others. We are also shown what the affect of different choices would have had on those lives as well. We are then asked questions about how much joy we felt in our lives and how much joy we brought to the lives of others, but not from a judgment perspective. Instead, those questions serve to help us learn, grow, and understand the power of our choices and free will so we can then use that knowledge to help us (and others) on our next journey. We are then given a choice to return to Earth to continue to learn and evolve to our highest self, or to balance some of our karma from the other side. My father proceeded to tell me that he chose the exit point he did because his soul had seen what I will be doing with my life. He had seen the impact I will have on millions of lives and felt he could help me more from that side than this side. (As an aside, my friend Pat knew nothing of the conversation my father and I had before he passed. No one knew that conversation except for my father and I). My father stayed by my side constantly for an entire year after he passed and for that reason (and still as I write this) he is with me whenever I call on him for his guidance, love, and support. Our loved ones never leave. Their soul never dies. They simply change worlds.

Life is about learning our lessons, living in a state of joy as often as possible and knowing we are never alone on our journey. God always does his part – now we need to do ours.

What will your choice be? Will you meet him halfway?

"In the long run, we shape our lives, and we shape ourselves. The process never ends until we die. And the choices we make are ultimately our responsibility." ~ Unknown

ACKNOWLEDGMENTS

There are so many people to thank and acknowledge I am not even sure where to begin. This book was 4 years in the making and at one point I never thought it was going to be finished. It was due to all of the people mentioned here, cheering me on and pushing me to my edge, as to why you are holding this book in your hand today.

First and foremost, my editor, Christopher Murray. Chris, I cannot begin to thank you enough. This book would never have come to fruition if it wouldn't have been for you, your wisdom and your kind way of pushing me to my edge to tap into my best. Your expertise and willingness to work with me "where I was" is what made my best come out in this book. You are amazing and a dear friend and I love you for sticking this through with me.

My two beautiful daughters, Lindsey and Natalie. As parents we think that our children are born to us so we can be their teachers and I can truly say my girls are a gift and were brought to me to be *my* teachers. Lindsey, your strength and fortitude to push through life no matter what happens around you is a gift I hope you will one day see in yourself. It is what makes you *you* and allows that inner light you have to shine so bright. Natalie, your tender and compassionate heart that wants to hug the world and make it all ok is a gift from the angels. Thank you for your poems which inspired me to live up to what you think of me as a person and as a Mom. I love you both with all of my heart.

My Mom, Genevieve Morth. Mothers and daughters always have a special bond that cannot be replaced. They serve as teachers for each other through the life experiences they share. Thank you Mom for being one of my greatest teachers. I love you.

My lifetime friend and "Bestie," Judy Maruna. Few people can say they have known someone from the age of 4 years old and are still friends but I am lucky to be able to say that about you. Even though we have never even lived in the same town for most of the time we have known each other, it brings peace to my soul to know you are the one person who will always, always be there to lend an ear, a gentle voice and encouragement when I need it most. You are one of the ones I want to make proud! Thank you and I love you so much.

Although he crossed to the other side in 2007, my father, Gary Morth, has been an inspiration to me after life as much as he was during life. His gentle and compassionate ways of living his life and graceful way he accepted death has been the "example point" I come back to no matter what happens in my life. You taught me about hope, faith and unconditional love. I love you and look forward to our meeting one day on "the other side." I love you Daddy.

My amazing assistant, Ruth Doubleday, who blows my mind every day by her greatness. Ruth, without you I would not have been able to focus as much time on this book as needed to make it great. You are amazing at what you do and a true gift in my life. Thank you so much for all you do for me every day!

I can go on and on but in short, thank you to all of the amazing teachers whom I have quoted in this book. You are the ones who I have read, listened to and studied that have helped mold me into the person that I am today. You are all brilliant teachers and a gift to this world. Thank you, thank you, thank you!

And to all of those friends who have cheered me on either through emails, Facebook and in whatever form you have found. Your encouragement and kind words mean more than you know and although you think I am your inspiration, the truth is, you are mine!

For more information about Chris Sopa and how to hire her to speak at your event:

Visit her website at www.chrissopa.com

Join her daily blog at www.chrissopa.wordpress.com

Email her at chris@chrissopa.com

Purchase and view other products by Chris Sopa International at www.chrissopa.com/products including:

Chakra Cleansing Meditation CD

CD's, MP3's and Videos for inspiration

Newsletters